An Introduction to

Exploring the Novel

For African Higher Education

An Introduction to

Exploring the Novel

For African Higher Education

Casimir K. Adjoe

EXCELLER BOOKS™
A GLOBAL PRESS

An Introduction to Exploring the Novel
For African Higher Education

Cover design by Exceller Books using resources from Pixabay.com

ISBN: 978-93-93734-54-9

First published in India in 2023 by Exceller Books
An Imprint of GE Group

Address: G1, Dream Apartment, Degree College Road, Belgharia, Kolkata, 700056, India

EXCELLER BOOKS™
A GLOBAL PRESS

www.excellerbooks.com

Dedication

The book is dedicated to my parents, John and Vincentia Adjoe, all my brothers and sisters, my friends, and all my beloved teachers.

'In man, creature and creator are united. In man, there is matter, fragment, excess, clay mud, madness, and chaos. But in man, there is also the creator, the sculptor, the hardness of the hammer, the divine spectator, and the seventh day – do you understand this antithesis?

- *Nietzsche: Beyond Good and Evil. 225*

Table of Contents

Preface

This introductory book discusses the essentials of understanding and interpreting the novel through the awareness of the basis of the construction of the literary piece upon language and social structural considerations and outlines. It is designed mainly for postgraduate students in African higher education exploring ways of approaching the interpretation and meaning-making of narratives, particularly novels, and those learning how to teach literature to students. It is rooted in the Sociology of Literature and Literary Theory. It seeks to answer a need of students of literature who think they have no specific method of approaching and articulating the interpretation, meaning-making, and relevance of texts even after all their prolific reading of literary works and studies and who, therefore, still feel at a loss, daunted and powerless when they stand face-to-face with texts and the world. This effort is to provide an introduction to articulating their literary studies and finding the means to make it practical for relevance as far as possible – a foothold to build upon.

The book explores how particular discourses relate to culture in the construction of the novel. This concern refracts into questions such as:

- How does the text create?
- How does the text organize knowledge? and
- How does the text stand in relation to ideology?

The first chapter examines the nature of language and discourse as shaped by human consciousness through conceptualisations. These conceptualisations, as Marx and

Mannheim observe, are bounded by their social-historical contexts.

The organisation of consciousness significantly relates to the positioning and occupation of the subject and the object. Hence, in examining the novel, we are also examining the position of the subject and object in relation to other constituent features such as text, reader, and content.

The second chapter traces the characteristics of ideology as it has developed in its social-historical framework from its eighteenth-century ideal of consciously developing 'a systematic analysis of ideas and sensations, their generation, combination, and consequences,' in its positive sense to its disqualification as illusory and negative by Marx, and subsequently to its neutralisation and pervasive character by persons such as Mannheim, and later Marxists like Althusser.

The third chapter explores the understanding that the acquired neutrality of ideology and its manifestation in the world vision of collective consciousness as discourse constitutes the most important element in the interpretation of the novel.

The fourth chapter explores the novels of Elisabeth Gaskell, particularly *Mary Barton* and *North and South*, to ascertain the thesis of the essence of the understanding and interpretation of the novel as a coherent structure fashioned through the conversation of discourses examining the social situation, structure and the potential transformative present in the light of the problematic hero and the existing alternative discourses. In Gaskell's novels, the discourses are carried out within the framework of the structure of the relationship between manufacturers and workers and between machines of manufacture and the principles of manufacture underpinned by the laissez-faire economics advocated by Adam Smith and the emergent questions of power, identity, and transformation.

I have used non-African novels for illustration:

- First, to acknowledge that literary works defy borders because they are about human consciousness, and
- Secondly, to highlight the pertinent problems of labour in African societies, which are not far from the experience of students.

Introduction

In this book, I shall discuss language, social structure, and the novel. It is an exercise in exploration and charting a course of understanding the text. As a result, I shall present a number of methodologies advanced for the analysis of literary work in the social-historical tradition. After the analyses and their principles, I shall use what appears to be the most accessible and relevant to examine a particular case, in this instance, Mrs. Gaskell's novels *Mary Barton* and *North and South*.

In *Mary Barton*, Gaskell examined the issues mainly from the worker's perspective. In *North and South*, she does so from the entrepreneur's perspective. My analysis will examine the issues related to this project mainly through these perspectives as the method articulated for interpretation shapes it.

According to Lucien Goldmann, the novel is the universe that brings together the dominating choice or ideology and its discourse in actual or possible combinations. When the novel steps outside this ideology or world-view and offers alternative discourses, it becomes subversive and potentially transformative. Consequently, I shall examine the nature of social structure as a cause or effect of language. The basic question which emerges from this is whether the novel does actually reflect the dynamics of the relationship between language and social structure.

My initial hypothesis is that the novel possesses what Goldmann calls 'a transformative value' with regard to social structure. But, how does it acquire this transformative character? Is it a consequence of a productive capacity as discourse or rather of its capacity as a model of social structure? In either direction, they inevitably evoke the relationship of the novel to culture.

Therefore, my purpose is to explore how a particular discourse, in this case, Mrs. Gaskell's novels, relates to culture. In general, this concern refracts into questions such as:

- How does the text create?
- How does the text organize knowledge?
- How does the text stand in relation to ideology?
- Is it, as Marxist critics contend, in opposition to the ideology and hence a form of free activity?

Or

- Is it staunchly part of ideology and ideology by itself?

In approaching this goal, I have considered several ways. I have considered an analysis by choice of and the concentration on a single literary theory. However, this would be at the cost of side-stepping the sociological component of literary works. I turned to sociological theory but was wary of the danger of excluding the literary perspectives of my discussions. Moreover, I could not even adopt a strictly philosophical analysis for the same reasons. Instead, I perceived a strong interrelationship between these various disciplines and their undoubted convergence in literary work, especially in the novel, which will be my main concern. From this standpoint, the choice of an interdisciplinary approach towards the engagement seems plausible as a way of reaching, as much as possible, a comprehensive understanding of the issues involved in the production of the text as a novel.

Nevertheless, to avoid the temptation of traversing beyond the scope of this book, I shall limit myself to the analysis of the significant structures of the novel. In this regard, I shall seek to make evident only some of the significant relations between the structures of the universe of the novel.

Consequently, after the theoretical examination of some of the structures relevant to constituting the method of analysis, I shall present a provisional analysis of the selection of a nineteenth-century novel as an exhibit. Nonetheless, I shall restrict the analysis in both content and form in accommodation to the text of choice for exploration. I believe it will, nevertheless, remain comprehensible and insightful.

Again, realizing the vast fields I have to chart, I propose to chart a course with heavier reliance on some sources than others. This will enable a degree of support around which I could crystalize the insights of the book. In this regard, Lucien Goldmann would provide me with the main compass to chart my access to the novel in the manner I wish to explore it.

1| What Is Discourse?

The novel operates within a space-time continuum. It is the textual manifestation of language and discourse. Ferdinand Saussure distinguished between langue and parole to differentiate between what people employ in thinking and conceptualising and what they employ in speech. This notion advances the perception that language and discourse are shaped by human consciousness through conceptualisations. Conceptualisation, however, does not take place in a vacuum. As some theorists such as Marx and Mannheim observe, it has a grounding in a social-historical framework.

Nonetheless, the novel can be perceived in different ways according to how it relates to consciousness. Thus, there is the possibility, for instance, of the conception and interpretation of the novel in the mode of a psycho-biographic analysis by means of psychoanalytic theory or in a purely immanent or phenomenological mode by means of hermeneutic theory or by 'the simple reflection of consciousness'1, or by means of structuralist theory. These represent various organisations of consciousness.

However, the organisation of consciousness bears a significant relation to the positioning and occupation of the subject and the object. Hence, in examining the novel, we are also examining the position of the subject and the object in relation to each other and to other constituent features such as text, reader, and content.

Deconstructionist theorists such as Jacques Derrida, refer to the different possibilities of organising consciousness and positioning the subject in relation to object, content, text, and reader to the extent of making them present or absent to produce a desired effect, meaning, identity, certainty, and truth, seek to debunk the processes of production by placing literary processes within their originating historical, cultural and ideological frameworks. He then questions their priority over other modes of organization to reveal the shifting limits of consciousness into particular kinds of knowledge, truth, and meaning to the exclusion of other kinds of processes of institutionalization.

In its process, deconstruction bares to the perception of the underlying assumptions and processes of institutionalizing the organization and seeks to reconvene other possibilities of organizing structures for meaning. The result is that deconstruction demonstrates that the literary text, like all other areas of organizing knowledge, meaning, and truth, undergoes a production process rather than being natural. The text can thus be considered a product.

Following Julia Kristeva's explication of the process, the epistemological conduct between subject and object results in textual production. The production process, nevertheless, does not itself end in the text. It continues between the text and the reader who makes sense of the text and its product and manufactures his/her own product in both partial correlation with and reproduction of the totality. A new fiction is consequently produced by the reader. An exploration of these disjunctions and conjunctions, presences and absences, and production and reproduction will constitute my engagement in the process of examining the thesis on whether language is a reflection of the social structure.

Language is a discourse. The process of discourse is the construction of meaning in the interpretation of reality. Already, the above assertion raises several questions, such as:

- What is reality?
- How do we know reality?
- Who constructs meaning – the individual or the collective?
- How is it constructed – consciously or unconsciously?

I shall endeavour to examine some of these facets of the nature of reality as examined variously in epochs and substance precisely because of their major role in determining the character, nature, quality, and direction of discourse. This is especially more so for the discussion of the ideological, the subjective, and the social or collective regarding the novel.

The analysis of reality has been undertaken in the realm of epistemology, rendering the question: What is knowledge, and how does one 'know'? Althusser credits philosophy with the production of specific discourses. The formulation of discourse through the analysis of reality has been carried out in such moulds as empiricism, rationalism, positivism, agnosticism, skepticism, idealism, and materialism. In all these approaches, the independence and correlation of the object to the subject (the known and the knower) are under scrutiny. Hindness and Hirst conceptualize the relationships are the examination between a disjunction and a correlation. Here the distinction between object and subject is withheld in favour of a preponderance of a distinction between discourse and an independent realm of the actual and potential objects about which discourse takes its proceedings. Hindess and Hirst's perspective assumes a suspended position because it is isolated from any foundation of the subject or knower. If it does, it has simply presupposed it without any illuminations of the foundations of the relationships. Therefore, what can be said for any view in this direction is that it takes place entirely within consciousness, but in whose and what consciousness remains unexplored.

Having highlighted the dangers of an analysis of reality entirely accommodated within consciousness, nevertheless devoid of an awareness of the 'carrier' or subject of consciousness, I now turn to a brief introduction to the philosophical streams whose attempts to analyse reality transcend this danger in a major way to provide alternative modes of analyses, gaining scope for the development of discourses and hence the possibility of examining either the independence or correlation of its elements and structure.

Philosophical developments in the seventeenth and eighteenth centuries concentrated on a rivalry between empiricism and idealism or rationalism. Empiricists like John Locke considered the subject a passive receptor of sense experience from an independent object. The mediator between the subject and the object is the consciousness which at birth is a tabula rasa. The mode of transmission of knowledge from the object to the subject is by a series of impressions constituting the secondary qualities of the original or primary qualities of the object itself. Knowledge is, thus, constituted, mediated, and evaluated by observable criteria. Consequently, statements of knowledge or discourse could only be constituted as observable entities. One, thus, cannot speak about what one has not seen. The definition of reality, being so independent of consciousness, is composed of a discourse compatible with its nature – a scientific discourse.

This means that the focus of discourse was on the external and the object rather than on the subject. Moreover, the implication of this position for the acquisition of knowledge is that it is only capable of being 'grasped' by a process of abstraction. The necessary subject can grasp only the essence of the reality or object outside themselves, which they otherwise attempt to apprehend. The consequence of such a process of abstraction and its complex combinations convert the status of discourse into a privileged acquisition, something given from the outside and 'grasped' inside the consciousness of the subject, who is the receptor and the receptacle. However, what is equally very important to understand is that in this theory, knowledge is essentially part of the object itself (and the subject receives knowledge of the object only at one remove from it).

The rival of empiricism is idealism. Idealism's major exponent was Berkeley, whose argument ran to the orientation that the material world exists only in our perceptions. What can be said immediately for this position is its assertion of the subject as primary in the relationship between the subject and the object. The constituency of the subject's apprehension of the material world is 'qualities.' The material world, in reality, does not exist. Reality consists of the perceptions of qualities according to the mental structures of the finite and infinite mind. The orderliness and regularity of the subject's ideas and perceptions constitute the laws of nature.

What are prominent in idealism's position are the pre-existing mental molds of the structures of the finite and the infinite and of order and regularity, which impose a definition on the perceptions and ideas reaching the subject's consciousness. Through such a conceptual framework, a process of abstraction is set in motion, even like that of empiricism.

However, the immense difference between idealism and empiricism remains in the emphasis on the subject and the object, respectively. On the side of idealism, knowledge of reality, which is the abstraction itself in consciousness, is the property of the knower or subject. In the construction of discourse in idealism, knowledge inevitably recognizes the privileged status of the subject and accordingly responds to it, basing itself on it.

Kant reconciled both positions of empiricism and idealism to produce a remarkable combination of rationalism. Kant conceived that unlike the empiricists (such as Hume) assert, the laws of nature, which are laws governing the reality of the independent external world, are not represented through sense impressions. Likewise, neither is it represented from the rationalist point of view (such as Descartes) in independently existing clear and distinct ideas. Instead, the mind gives its own laws to nature - mind is the law-giver to nature. The concepts of the mind determine the structure of what comes to it, hence what the subject knows. The concept implies that the subject lives in a world of their own making. However, the idea of the subject constructing their own world through the medium of consciousness is modified by the fact that they can fashion such construction on the phenomena or appearances only, for they cannot know reality as it is independent of themselves and their concepts, that is as Kant calls them, 'things–in– themselves.'

The subject is incapable of knowing reality owing to the nature of the mind and of reality itself. Kant posits that the mind is neither empty (a tabula rasa) nor passive. Instead, it is an active interpreter of the external world through the senses. Hence, simple reaction and recording memory are not its pertinent duties. The process of knowing and interpreting the world is carried through twelve categories or pure concepts, which are a priori, that is, logically prior to experience. These pure concepts are organised under four necessary relationships: quantity, quality, relation, and modality. The classification of these items may be represented in a table as follows:

Quantity	Quality	Relation	Modality
Unity	Affirmation	Substance-accident	Possibility
Plurality	Negation	Cause-effect	Actuality
Totality	Limitation	Casual Reciprocity	Necessity [2]

In their relationship with experience, they precede it in the form of consciousness and are presupposed by it. Secondly, the experience cannot alter or modify them. Instead, they offer the only means of understanding experience. Thirdly, they are the characteristic structure of any consciousness, hence universal. This set the basis for inter-subjective understanding, discursiveness, and relationships.

Fourthly, they are necessary for the organisation and unification of knowledge, for without them, experience would not be possible except only as a flux of sense experience and knowledge.

Fifthly, the distinction between phenomena or appearance and 'things–in–themselves' (the essence) is thereby determined since only the essence of reality can be contemplated. The concepts determine the essence.

Kant's analysis is of great importance in many directions as it has probably appeared so far. However, of greatest significance, perhaps, is the position it gives to the subject in relation to reality. Reality is indeed a product of the subject's consciousness. It also depicts the nature of reality as structural because reality is non-existent except in accordance with the structuration offered by the prior structures of the subject's consciousness. The implications of these postulations are that the product of the subject's consciousness in the appearance manifested through consciousness is an exact replica or reproduction of the external object or experience. Owing to the ceding of a direct relationship between subject and object towards an ordering and structuring of perception, subjects can only act in relation to the product of their own structurations, which becomes inevitably naturalised and constituted as the essence of the perceived real or external objects.

The entire relationship and analysis engender profound implications for discourse, for the nature of discourse will be determined not by knowledge of the external objects outside it but by the structures of consciousness. This is as true for science as for any other domain of discourse – the concepts of the mind determine the laws of nature.

Of course, these concepts crystalise and become formalised through reification. Reification of concepts and appearances leads to relation to them 'as if' they were the real world. Perhaps this is best illuminated by Nietzsche in his discussion on discourse. In his treatise, 'Human all too Human,' he described the constitution of language as putative. He observed that:

> *The significance of language for the evolution of culture lies in this that mankind set up in language a separate world, a place it took to be so firmly set that standing upon it, it could lift the rest of the world off its hinges and make itself master of it. To the extent that man has for long ages believed in the concepts and names of things as inaetenae veritates, he has appropriated to himself that pride by which he raised himself above the animal: he really*

> *thought that in language, he possessed knowledge of the world. The sculptor of language was not so modest as to believe that he was only giving things designations he conceived rather than with words; he was expressing supreme knowledge of things; language is, in fact, the first stage of the occupation with science*
> *... Logic, too, depends on presuppositions with which nothing in the real world corresponds, for example, on the presuppositions that there are identical things, that the same thing is identical at different points in time: but this science came into existence through the opposition belief (that such conditions do obtain in the real world). It is the same with mathematics, which would certainly not have come into existence if one had known from the beginning that there was in nature no exactly straight line, no real circle, no absolute magnitude.* [3]

The putative character of language or discourse endows it with a faculty for imagination and manipulation. Again Nieztsche describes this faculty as the imagination in terms of infinity. By this faculty, the subject creates, recreates, interprets, and makes meaningful or meaningless projects and errs or produces an effect. Through the activity of the imagination, a whole world and existence are brought to life, and hence, there is the possibility of an infinity of perspectives. He posits this view in 'The Gay Science':

> *How far the perspectival character of existence extends or whether it has any other character at all, whether an existence without interpretation, without 'meaning,' would not become 'meaningless,' whether, on the hand, all existence is not an interpreting existence - this, as is only reasonable, cannot even be determined even by the most assiduous and painfully conscientious analysis and self-examination of the intellect: since in the course of this analysis, the human intellect cannot avoid viewing itself in its perspectival forms and only in them. We cannot see around our own corner: it is a hopeless piece of curiosity to want to know what could exist for other species of intellect and perspective: for example, whether any kind of being could experience time in a reverse direction or alternately forward and backward (which could posit a different direction of life and a different conception of cause and effect). However, I think today we are at least far from the ludicrous immodesty of decreeing only from out of the corner. The world has rather once again become for us 'infinite': in so far as we cannot reject the possibility that it contains in itself infinite interpretations...*[4]

At this turn of imagination, manipulation, and the possibility of infinity in perspectives, discourse assumes the tendency of Organising itself according to the definite role and function in the form of ideology. Nietzsche denounces it as 'decreeing from out the corner' for the genesis of other perspectives.

Ideology developed from the formalisation or, more adequately, what we may call the naturalisation of a single perspective as the genesis of all other perspectives and interpretations. Consequently, ideology imposes a structure on all reality, the structure deriving from the perception of reality in relation to subject and object and the meditating medium of consciousness. Thus, positivism, for example, develops from the empiricist position to assert only the describable and what can be designated for approval as 'what exists,' in order words, the state of existence. Discourse in this light tended to be centered on materialistic analysis. The novel, for instance, would have to be 'realistic' in the sense of the description of the real situation developing outside the author, real events, objects, and places. A diary or a journalistic form of the novel was thereby likely to be projected as the natural discourse and norm, such as in classic realist novels. On the other hand, counterpart positivism can put rationalism into agnostic positions, which assert the 'unknowability' of the real, the potential of the subject to create their own existence and to structure it. Existentialist discourses such as Sartre and structuralist discourses can be nurtured in this mould. While the positivistic orientation may make claims of 'truth' and hence of an undeniable monolith of description or interpretation of the discourse, the latter positions may offer more flexibility in the toleration of the multiplicity of interpretations and explanations, except that this all ought to take off from the pre-established basis of their perspectives. Sartre illuminates my position quite well in describing the influence of 'extreme' situations' on the writers in 1947, that is, during the post-war period, parallel to the writers of the eighteenth-century. He writes that:

> *Since we were situated, the only novels we could dream of were novels of situation without internal narrators or all-knowing witnesses. In short, if we wished to give an account of courage, we had to make the techniques of the novel shift from Newtonian mechanics to generalized relativity. We had to people our books with minds that were half-lucid and half-overcast. We might consider some of them with more sympathy than others, but none of them would have a privileged point of view either upon the event or upon itself. We had to prevent creatures whose reality would be the tangled and contradictory tissue of one evaluation of all the other characters, including themselves, and who could never decide from within whether the change of their destinies came from their own efforts, from their own fault or from the course of the universe. Finally, we had to leave doubts, expectations, and the unachieved throughout our works, leaving it to the reader to conjecture for themselves by giving them the feeling, without giving them or letting them guess our feeling, that his view of the plot and the characters was merely one amongst many.*[5]

Discourse, by so doing, consists of a blueprint, a pattern dictating the shape, direction of its expansion or contraction, etc. This blueprint is the seed of discourse that sprouts and blossoms in imagination and textual representation (in the novel too): this blueprint or pattern is the ideology behind discourse, from which it does not deviate despite the variations which might be constructed upon it as Sartre points out. Sartre also makes a very important representation in depicting the author as an artist or 'creator.' Here the author is given the privilege of the subject who creates, the dominant agent who imagines his creation and fashions it according to a definite structure selected from among many others existing as possibilities. Ideologies abound.

Nevertheless, as we have seen before, Kant's idea is privileged structures of the mind over the subject or author. Like the structuralists, therefore, the ideology upon which discourse stands is what I might call 'the fashioning agents' and the code of the text and the imagination as circumscriber, not the subject per se. The imagination of the subject is unequivocally the reproduction of the grand structure presupposed by the mind. From this, there can hardly be a relative perspective of the structure of the subject except for miniature reflections of the subject itself. They are determined to produce the structure, unlike in the former case where a reproduction of the structure results yet is still very accommodating of other perspectives, acknowledging some independence from itself (because of the subject's amenability). I shall return to this subject of reproduction of the structure later in my exposition, especially in relation to Goldman and his mentors, such as Lukacs. But now, let me turn to another important strain in Sartre's passage. We will discuss Sartre's situation of the analysis in a historical context. Time and space and their arrangement produce a great impact on discourse. The novel of situation makes its appearance within a particular historical continuum, the post-war period, 1947, and relates to objects and events. The codes or ideologies which guided the subject or authors of this period were based on situations. The construction of a character to fit into and to enact the conditions of their human situation, or the external situation as it has been rendered, was given to the imagination, capable of nurturing or fashioning out different kinds of perspective, albeit based on the same code of relatively in pertaining to the novel must presuppose the basic code to ensure a relevant explanation to the novel's unity.

Thus, all novels engender a code, consciously or unconsciously. The code gives the imagination a form that composes the various forms or genres of texts and fiction, e.g., the epic, the romantic novel, the existentialist, the industrial, the modernist, or the post-modernist novel.

In the historical sphere, fiction embarks on dealing with the past. The question arises: Is such a relationship a direct representation, reflection, or mirroring of the totality of the past or simply a selective reconstruction of a world that does not exist anymore, or rather the creation of an entirely new world, alive and worthy of being acted upon? Another question arises in relation to the sociological character, the relationship between the text and the world of events within which the text is existing and/or is being described.

Does the text merely reflect the world (and relationships) within which it is living in the present, or does it create its own world different from it? If it does create a different world, how does it proceed, and what relationship does it bear to the concrete existence of the reader especially? Does the text authorise in any form an intellectual journey and a concrete relationship to both its content and form? All these bear a special relationship to the definition of the text in its self-perception as emphasising form or content. The emphasis on form or content is itself derivative from its ideological code, built upon a subject-object preference or consciousness preference.

Discussing the narrative to rediscover the seminal pattern through a study of the structure and the functioning of its major constituent parts, the sediments of its construction, and the contributory influences and trends fusing into the parts which were synthesized to constitute the whole is the task of deconstruction. Such endeavour asserts the possibility of demythologising and desacralising forms and their imperatives as 'the FORM' or 'the truth.' The possibility of such endeavour and its effects has occasioned the entitlement of the era of the endeavour as the era of the 'end of ideology,' e.g., Louis Althusser.

In one sense, this is true because of the effect of debunking ideology in lifting off the strictures of knowledge and revealing infinite possibilities. In another sense, the end of ideology cannot be ascertained because debunking or unmasking the pretensions of truth does not necessarily kill it off. However, it can be ascertained that ideology has definite connections with the privileged classes, its beliefs, and values or with the state and its mechanisms.

It is only in light of the universal transformation in society at large that any claims can be made for the beginning of the end of a particular kind of ideology. Or in another sense, referring to the other kinds of ideology that confront the dominant one, though they may abandon a grand structural confrontation as a programme designed towards transformation, nevertheless, their existence as identifying elements for the possibilities of change and internal reform opportunities are still as potent as ever. Looking at it from the point of view of the novel, only when the novel serves a transformative role by variegating or breaking up the power of such dominant beliefs and values systems and mechanisms and liberates itself from them to represent the values of the totality of society can the claim be justified. In fact, later in the process, I shall be examining the entire spectrum through Lucien Goldmann's perspective on the subject. However, for the moment, I propose to examine the concept of ideology in more detail

2 | Ideology and the Novel

Estut de Tracy invented the term 'ideology' toward the end of the eighteenth century to designate his attempt to create 'a science of ideas', which would form the basis and methodology for approaching knowledge and the affairs of planning all human endeavour practically for the improvement of man. It derived its inspiration and material from the tenets of the Enlightenment and its aspirations. It would rely on the 'systematic analysis of ideas and sensations, their generation, combination, and consequences.'[1] In this sense, ideology was purported to be 'positive, useful, and susceptible of rigorous exactitude.'[2]

By the beginning of the nineteenth century, Napoleon Bonaparte had acceded to the throne of France. The politics of Napoleon and the monarchists conflicted with the liberalism of Estut de Tracy's mode of interpreting reality and its association with republicanism, where a campaign of formulating an entirely different or alternative method of analysing reality and application to political reality was initiated. It was designed to denigrate Tracy's methods of analysis, consigning it under the connotation of an erroneous body of ideas that remained impracticable in relation to the realities of political life. It stood out thus as a set of abstract and illusory ideas.

Consequently, the enlightenment ideals of a 'rational understanding of the world and of the rational self-determination of human beings'[3] became perceived as inadequate in the determination of human affairs, and thus ideology acquired a negative sense, precipitating the tendency to ideology suspiciously.

Kant distinguished between essence and appearance in the possibility of the subject's reception and knowledge of the world. The subject can only 'grasp' appearances of things-in-themselves, i.e., they receive knowledge of reality only at a second remove from themselves. However, they give structure to reality and thereby create knowledge. Such rationalism forms the basis of the enlightenment subject and knowledge. Estut de Tracy's ideological construction, now discredited as illusory, did take nurture from this root. In doing so, the rationalists had over-emphasised the privilege of the subject and had overlooked the other side of Kant's assertions that the subject does not apprehend things as they are in themselves, which means that the subject interprets or structures things quite differently from what they are in themselves and thus creates their own world, which in effect could be different still if interpreted or structured in another way, combination, or by some other subject. This raises a potential question about relative and solipsism, which Kant tries to avoid by postulating the universalisation and naturalisation of various subjects' structurations through what is known as 'inter-subjectivity.'

The vessel of universalisation and naturalisation of knowledge, as Terry Eagleton notes in his discussion of the aesthetic, is symbolisation, which under bourgeoisie custody, is firmly grounded in ideology. However, Eagleton, like many others, avoids regarding this bourgeoisie ideology through symbolisation in a negative light.

What Napoleon's disdain of 'ideology' did to its condition was to provide an alternative oppositional trademark to its hitherto positive and useful status. The alternative oppositional position was adopted by Karl Marx, whose formulations of the term and its meaning have been the most notable among scholars, albeit incoherently constructed by Marx himself. Nevertheless, ideology has also been given much more of a neutral status in the views of other scholars after Marx. These include even Marxists such as Lukacs, Goldmann, and Eagleton and some non-marxists like Karl Mannheim, who albeit borrowed from Marx. However, before the further exposition of the neutral status of ideology, I shall make a slight detour through the basis of the Marxist ideas on ideology.

The Marxist ideas also had roots in Kant, but much more so in Hegel's rationalism and idealism. Hegel adopted Kant's concept of the structuration of reality by the mind, hence 'the real is the rational, and the rational the real.'[4]

The subject thereby more or less perceives from their point of view. Nevertheless, they constructed his point of view within a dialectic in which the subject as an individual finds itself only as a part of a totality that is constantly in dynamic motion and transformation. The privilege that the subject thus enjoyed in Kant's rationalism as creator is consequently lessened considerably, reduced to a single thread. The subject is reduced to a function of the absolute mind, which is a unified totality of all rational truth. Absolute mind spans all areas of experience and knowledge and is the organiser of all its diversity into a coherent unity. By this character, absolute mind is a unity-in-diversity and a 'one that comprises the many.'[5]

Marx's view, to a great extent, coincided with Hegel's world-view. However, when transposed into the social-historical realm, he found the duality between the metaphorical representation and the empirical or material intolerable. Appearance and essence had to be brought together into one the same thing. He fell out with the young Hegelians precisely because of the reluctance on their part to perceive reality deeper in its essence by clearly identifying rational ideas with existence. The young Hegelians, for Marx, remained in a state of rational and illusory suspension, completely divorced from the processes of the real world and therefore impractical and ineffectual. As Thompson renders it, 'the young Hegelians oppose ideas with ideas, they fight phrases, and as a result, they leave the world unchanged.' [6] The young Hegelians, by the orientation of their system of analysis, had constituted ideas into an autonomous theoretical doctrine, efficacious on their own. This orientation of perceiving meaning was demeaning for Marx, who designated all ideology as identifying within this category, just as Napoleon had denounced those who practised the Enlightenment ideals of rational sovereignty and its construct by Estut de Tracy as 'ideologues.'

Translated into socio-historical discourse, Marx desired it to be perceived that 'the forms of consciousness of human beings are the manifest determination of the material conditions of their life.'[7] Hence manifestations of reasoning and the production of ideas are not self-determined or self-determined. In the same vein, they do not prescribe the course of history. They are instead like Hegel's unity-in-diversity of Absolute Mind, a constituent part of the collective human effort to effect a means of subsistence. Thus, ideas are not causes but effects.

Marx explains the genesis of ideology by means of the division of labour. As the revolution of society advanced from 'herd consciousness,' it began to acquire a multiplicity of differentiations.

One of the differentiations was that between the material and the mental. In terms of labour, these would be described as the division of material labour and mental labour. Individuals who engaged in mental labour began to imagine their products in the forms of theoretical frameworks such as theology, philosophy, ethics, etc., to assume a life of their own, identifying them with the 'real.' The autonomy accorded mental products invented from here.

Those responsible for mental labour had assumed the illusory for real. Thus, Marx suggests an inadvertent self-deceit among intellectuals investing their reasoning and ideas with autonomy. Those ideas are what he regarded as ideology. Instead of ideology in this regard, something else must be substituted. What is most suitable for the comprehension of human ideas and endeavour must begin with the specific study of society and its history to discover the real conditions of their production in their circumstances.

In another relation, Marx and Lenin connected ideology with domination. As regarded by the authors in 'The German Ideology,' domination was restricted to conduct between social classes.

According to them, 'The ideas of the ruling class are in every epoch the ruling ideas, i.e., which is the ruling material force of society, is at the same time its ruling intellectual force.'[8] We must note that already the ideas of the ruling class are ideological. Being ideological, then, in Marx's sense, they are illusory. That they are presumed for the construction of economic production and its consequent relationships means that the relations of production are by themselves illusory too. Nevertheless, the contradiction which surfaces in Marx's thought here pertains to the fact that he had already remarked on the impracticality of illusory ideas and had, by that, explained the ineffectuality of the young Hegelians. The question, therefore, arises about how it has been possible for the ruling class to actualise their illusory ideas into real social-historical situations as relations of economic production. However, the main concern of my examination of this aspect of Marx's concept of ideology is the connection with domination. However, Marx explains the relation of domination by saying that the ideology of the dominant class articulates its ambitions, and this fact does not represent the real nature and character of the relations – it misrepresents it. To unmask this misrepresentation, one must investigate the forms of consciousness behind the development of the economic conditions of production. From this picture, one may glean the mechanism of socio-historical change and notice that the underlying forms of consciousness guiding the relations within these processes belong to the ruling classes whose interests and ambitions are represented in it. Relations such as private property are typical of such forms of consciousness which, although illusory, have been reified, sanctified, and universalised to accord them a natural profile. The transparency of social relations in its illusory forms is the consequence of the emergence of capitalism. In capitalism, the subordinate classes have been able to perceive their position, its artificiality, and illusory foundations better. The task of the subordinates remains to sweep away the 'false consciousness' initiated and sustained by ideology, the symbol of ruling class interests, for a more truly universal interest based on that of the proletariat. Consequently, Marx restricts ideology to the representation of the class interest, which ultimately serves as the instrument of ruling class domination and its sustenance.

In this regard, it is 'false consciousness' devoid of any real logical basis and apparatus. It is only maintained through concealment and manipulation.

However, subsequent writers have discovered a neutral side of ideology. Ideology may not necessarily be negative nor positive, and the relations that arise from it, as Marx wholly consigned it. Ideology may indeed possess some degree of autonomy and efficacy. As Thompson expresses it,

'They constitute symbols and slogans, customs and traditions which move people or hold them back, propel them or constrain them' (in such a way that we cannot think of these symbolic constructions as solely determined by, and fully explicable in terms of the economic conditions of production.)[9] The rendition of ideology in this form is what might appropriately be called symbolic form. Symbolic forms are much more elaborated upon by Max Weber in his interpretative and hermeneutical rationalisation of the causes of the divergencies in the development of societies in Protestant ethics and the spirit of capitalism. His approach removed the negative flavour of Marx's conception of the term in its qualification of ideology. Weber removed the particularity of dominant and dominating ideas to social classes and especially to ruling classes alone, demonstrating that these could be located within any section of the society guided in his attitudes and behaviour by a coherent code of ideas and commitment.

Both Lenin and Lukacs were Marxists, but they had, nevertheless, begun to neutralise ideology, separating it from its proletariat's self-organisation. Ideology now ceases to be preserved as the exclusive instrument of the dominant classes, being now seen as amenable in the hands of the cross-section of classes and groups within society for the integration of its ideas, its organisation, and operation for functional effectivity. Thus, ideology now serves class interests, not only the asymmetrical ok interests of the dominant class alone.

Mannheim and Lukacs converged in recognising the importance of locating thoughts or ideas in history and treating them as offsprings of the socio-historical processes and context. Mannheim's concern was nevertheless to investigate the social conditions which give rise to knowledge and thought. He proposed the total conception of ideology as the methodology for this study. This proposition postulates the study of the total structure of the mind of the period, i.e., approaching it through the study of history or of a socio-historical group: that is, approaching through the study of particular units or blocks, such as class. From this methodology can be grasped the Weltanschauung or world-view of the group or the period under study. It may also become quite clear how essential this world-view is intimately a product of the socio-historical processes of life situation (sitz im leben) of the period. This outcome is essentially collective. We can distinguish this from the particular conception of ideology, the negative kind described by Marx, which is responsible for cultivating false consciousness. This is individual and unrelated to social contexts. Therefore, according to Mannheim's formulation:

> *'Ideology may be regarded as the interwoven systems of thought and modes of experience which are conditioned by social circumstances and shared by groups of individuals including those engaged in ideological analysis.'*[10]

With Mannheim, ideology assumes the characteristics of a research method in social and intellectual history for analysing social factors influencing general thought as well as the author's own. Already in assigning ideology to the domain of the collective, springing from socio-historical processes and groups, Mannheim subjects the individual and the subject to the collective processes of context. It is the same kind of decentring of the subject as the Marxists are inclined to ascribe to the individual within the relations of Production. Nevertheless, Mannheim's concept goes further in circumscribing the fact that even all relations of production can be studied within social-historical processes and periods. This approach raises the prospect that relations of production are not monolithically similar in all epochs and social circumstances, nor are they completely unalterable or uninfluenced by external or internal circumstances as the Marxist approach seems to suggest in its structural absolutism. Goldmann certainly falls in line with Mannheim's conception and understanding of totality in its social, historical, internal, and external influences and the resultant alterability of social circumstances. It also constitutes the enabling principle of the existence of possibilities, albeit still accommodated within the totality of the social-historical dialectic. At least before the writing of 'Towards a sociology of the novel,' this was his position. In 'Towards a sociology of the novel,' although he still believed in the social-historical and other influences, he thought that the stage of development hitherto had lost its momentum for creativity and transformation, so characteristics of past epochs because the level of consciousness which existed then has now been whittled away by the reification and fetishisation of every product in the market economy.

Consciousness does not possess the ability to be other than it is anymore. The author, within this circumspection, thus no longer represents an individual but a product of the market and its consciousness while the possibility which existed are no longer available to them.

In his 'Ideology and Utopia,' Mannheim presents a delineation of the boundaries of ideology and the possibilities it has the potential to sustain. Within the same projected vision, he attempted the delineation of a transcendence of the domain of ideology in both extension and the range of possibilities engendered through the concept of utopia.

However, the differentiation between ideology and utopia became ambiguous as their likeness became more evident, except for the unlimited possibilities existing within utopia than within ideology. Nevertheless, he gives privilege to utopia as the more transcendent form of a collective consciousness of a particular group capable of generating symbolic forms which can attain concrete social historical satisfaction for a while until the situation becomes too tight for survival or for comfort. Then the situation warrants another development and projection by the collectivity involved to pursue and satisfy. Hence, in the case of ideology, the world-view, which has been generated by a particular period through symbolic forms to attain some particular objectives, is restricted. It is restricted because it is tailored precisely, almost scientifically, to fit the objectives as precisely as they have been designed. Since it is impossible to achieve these objectives as precisely as they have been designed, the group soon finds it necessary to define another world view and its symbolic forms. This process continues successively as in a spiral and yet every time achieves its stated objectives and world view.

In one sense, a picture of this sort discredits ideology as very limited, almost giving it back the negative flavour bestowed on it by Marx.

Perhaps that is precisely the point that Mannheim comes back to, although he had initially rejected it. Hence, to avoid this pitfall, he makes a distinction. Nothing the basis of symbolic forms and world views as not acceptable, he classifies a particular perception of ideas (which includes the pursuit of narrow objectives in the interests of a particularly privileged group) and their construction in the category of negative practice and still labels them by the name of ideology. On the other hand, ideas or concepts representing the collective consciousness and participating in it are regarded more in the light of their representational credentials and extended vision to merit a privileged position of neutrality. These are termed 'utopia.' The world views and possibilities which derive from this realm are warranted their credibility.

The neutrality of ideology in its description as 'utopia' is apparently a major influence on Goldmann's conception of collective consciousness and the possibilities it engenders. It is also responsible for the novelist's rootedness in the social-historical sphere as well as the nucleus around which it took off onto the artificial construction of a new world view; which is, in fact, the projection of a combination of the realities of the collective consciousness and several or selected possibilities to create a new type of possible existence.

The neutrality of ideology was also described under the auspices of total ideology. That is, in all characteristics, 'total ideology' and utopia are one and the same entity.

In this sense, J.B. Thompson's description aptly illustrates the trend observing that:

Neutral conceptions are those which purport to characterise phenomena are necessarily misleading,

> *Illusory or aligned with the interests of any group, ideology, according to the neutral conceptions, is one aspect of social life (or form of social enquiry) among others and is no more or less attractive or problematic than any other.*
>
> *Ideology may be present, for example, in every political programme, irrespective of whether it aspires to the transformation or the preservation of social order as it is to dominant*

> *groups in their defence of the status quo. Like military hardware or tactical know-how, ideology may be a weapon that is orientated towards victory but towards no particular victor since it is, in principle, available to any combatant who has the resource and skills to acquire and employ it.*[11]

Having established neutrality for ideology in this form, it assumes the credentials of diffusiveness since it is an aspect of social life which consequently can be converted by any social group at any level for the organisation of its own programmes and their projection within the totality of the society. This means that ideology cannot be confined to a social category and its interests, constituting it as their monopoly, for example, by Marx in relation to the bourgeoisie. However, it does mean that social class does not comprise the sole framework within which to analyse the operation of ideology and that it assumes a plurality of frameworks such as gender, race, ethnic groups, individuals, and the state, nation-states, blocs of nation-states, regions, family, education, and other kinds of institutions which can also form the basic framework of organisation for any social group.

When analysed in relation to inequality and domination, any of these frameworks could compose the construct upon which such relations have been established and subsequently sustained. Such analysis is possible because each of these factors is capable of creating asymmetrical relationships between the dominant groups exercising them and the others organising themselves on a different or less successful model or, more importantly, on a less powerful organisation of symbolic forms. The concept of symbolic forms is essential in course of the explanation and analysis of asymmetrical relationships (i.e. inequality and domination). Symbolic forms compose meaning which is ingrained in the social context and homogenises the interpretation of the social world. They manifest in such forms as utterances and expressions, spoken or written, visual or sound images, or in a combination of all of these. In a sense, they are the instrumental embodiment of ideology. These referential instruments function to communicate specific types of relations through the provision, maintenance, and reproduction of meaning and interpretations which are consumed within the social context. The asymmetrical relations of domination engendered in these communications are thereby established and maintained as a natural or normative phenomenon. On the other hand, these symbolic constructions can be employed to subvert existing symmetrical relations of domination. The dual function of symbolic forms seemingly places them in a neutral role, being amenable to employment both for narrower ideological pursuits and for their subversion. The communication of these takes five main forms as outlined by J.B. Thompson: legitimation, dissimulation, unification fragmentation, and reification. Each of these processes possesses its own means of organising and shaping the transmission of its contents.

Legitimation, as a symbolic form, organizes itself in the forms of rationalisation, universalistion, and narrativisation. Legitimisation derives from Marx Weber's analysis of authority and authorisation through principles of rationality, the traditional, and charismatic modes. Therefore, legitimation establishes the grounds for acceptance of the contents being posited on the basis of a certain authority other than just the ideological content. The ideological content is now conveyed upon a set of reasoned-out arguments to provide justification for its support in the form of a ratioalisation of its nature and presentation. After disregarding its progenitors and its particularity, it is further postulated for acceptance in symbolic patterns suggesting that these contents are true for everyone everywhere and at every time, thus establishing their universalism. Moreover, they are not simply left to stand on their own – they are made dynamic and diffused through narrativisations; that is, they are more ubiquitous through their rendition into stories, films, history, documentaries, and novels. From this point of view, the novel is one means and forms among many others that is employed by symbolism to legitimate the relationships preferred by a particular group within a social group and a social context, presumably practiced by itself and seeking to protect it for all others within the wider social context. Furthermore, as authorized through the processes of rationalistion and universalisation, the novel acquires a quality of ahistoricity, transcending its time dimension since it is accorded none. It is thereby designated as timeless since it is perceived as symbolising perfectly rational and universal values in its descriptive relationships. Thus consciously or unconsciously, legitimation invests the novel with an eternal hegemonic value or 'truth.' Consequently, what the novel does in this framework is the reflection of society 'as it should always be.' Many of the classical realist novels bear the characteristic in a very distinctive fashion in the depiction of the value systems, norms, and conventions of society – which are really the values of a particular section of the society, such as the aristocracy, e.g., Jane Austen.

Ideology may employ dissimulation to communicate itself functionally in symbolic forms such as displacement, euphemisation, and tropes. In displacement, it may transfer either the negative or positive attributes of an object or individual onto another in an attempt to invest it with the same response or reactions in relation to the former. Euphemisation is specifically designed to evoke a positive valuation. Hence actions, institutions, and social relations are described or redescribed in very acceptable terminology away from some less acceptable formulation or symbolisation of it. Moreover, dissimulation may be accomplished through tropes. This involves the use of facilities of figurative language such as metaphor, synecdoche, and metonymy. Ideology may operate as a hidden hand behind the operation of the communication involved in the text of the novel. In this way, the novel may be functioning to communicate the world view of a particular group without any specific or direct reference to it while, in fact, subtly doing so. Meanwhile, unification as a symbolic form offers another mode of presenting ideology in an acceptable garb. It may be achieved through standardisation. Standardisation appeals to the need for a collective identity in a mixed or quite mixed environment. It establishes a common framework by which ideas and symbols can be shared and understood by collectivity. Standard symbolic forms and significations are thus bounded by legitimacy and collective identity, thus dissembling the genesis of the ideas and their new situations of collective consciousness and identity, which are represented in symbolisations of unity. This means that new symbolic forms representing unity, collectivity, and identity pick up the currency and are vigorously disseminated. On the other hand, instead of unification, ideology may employ the mould of fragmentation to fortify or maintain itself within a collectivity. This can be carried through the channels of such symbolic forms as differentiation and expurgation of the other.

Through differentiation, it constructs significations and symbolic forms which lay emphasis on the distinctions, differences, and divisions between individuals and groups, resulting in the creation of in-group and out-group conditions. The in-group and out-group symbolisations may be advanced to their extremes, conducting what can be termed 'the expurgation of the other,' where an individual or group is targeted and portrayed in diverse antagonistic significations and symbolic forms as evil, harmful, and threatening.

Merleau-Ponty refers to this approach as the principle of reducing the other to an object (to make one's objectives more attainable by lessening the conditions for scruples).

Reification is another way in which ideology functionalises itself. Its favorite manner of operation here is to isolate a transitory historical state, atomise it and give it a treatment representative of a permanent, natural, and eternal phenomenon. Its various symbolic forms include naturalisation, externalisation, and nominalisation or passivisation. Thus by naturalisation, a state of affairs that rightfully must be located within the creation of social-historical circumstances is divested of these origins and reinvested with a claim that they are natural and so symbolised as such, e.g., the division of labour between the sexes. Another dimension of this can be formulated through externalisation. In this sphere only the historical dimension of the state of affairs is abandoned, nevertheless creating the impression that these phenomena - be they institutions or events, are permanent and ever recurring, corresponding to which symbolic forms are constructed. However, the dominating ideas can be put forth conveniently through the manipulation of grammar and syntax. In nominalisation, phrases or parts of sentences can be converted into nouns or noun clauses, which thus stall the poignancy and package the entire meaning into what the author projects into it or determines it to be. Alternatively, through passivisation, verbs are rendered in the passive form instead of their active forms, thus causing a blunting of the context of things and events. This means that things and events are no more endowed with actors or with their agency. Instead of processes, that is, the dynamics and relations between things and objects, only the things and objects are left on their own, obviously without any dynamism. They are cast into what Hirst and Hindness call 'distinctions,' as distinguished from the processes and relations they ought to characterise. From the description of the various symbolic forms constituting the methodological tools of ideology in sustaining and establishing itself or subverting some other existing rivals, it becomes clear that the symbolic form defines, streamlines, stabilises and mobilises meaning towards a social function. Nevertheless, what ought to be taken into account are the following:

- To determine precisely what purpose they serve, especially with respect to whether they assist the substance of relations of domination or subvert them,
- The specific contexts in which they are produced,
- Who the producers are,
- Who the consumers are, and
- How they are consumed

From the attributes of the symbolic forms so far, another thing becomes clear – ideology invests any literacy piece or activity with a voice. The novel also shares this voice. The novel employs the language of symbolic forms and thus reflects the orientations of the sustaining idea of society. Goldmann asserts, like Adorno that any great piece of literature must have taken root from a particular and identifiable ideological collective consciousness or group. The argument becomes particularly strong because of the absolute importance of the trans-individual subject in relation to the supremacy of the whole over the parts and as the realm where the identity of the author is defined in the position it holds in relation to the total social-historical context. Thus, in 'The Hidden God,' Goldmann affirms the position of the author as a partial actor within the whole, one who, as it were, captures the life and aspirations of their group and its development through '...any great literary or artistic work is the expression of a world vision. This vision is the product of a collective consciousness that reaches its highest expression in the mind of a poet or a thinker. The expression that his work provides is then studied by the historian, who uses the idea of a world vision as a tool that will help him to deduce two things from the text:

The essential meaning of the work he is studying, and

The meaning that the individual and partial elements take on the work is looked at as a whole. [12]

Before we resume the discussion of the transindividual subject and the partial in relation to the whole in constituting any literary work, especially in the novel, let me sum up the discussion so far concerning the relationship of the novel to the symbolic forms. I have analysed the works of Marx, Mannheim, Lukacs, Foucault, Thompson, Merleau-Ponty and Goldmann, Adorno, and Bourdieu and, from the relationships, have determined that – the novel participates in language and employs the language of the symbolic forms in the codification of its message. It, thus, reflects the orientation of the sustaining idea of the symbolic forms and, therefore, the universally accepted meanings and understanding of the society as long as it must seek to communicate itself to a particular group in the society in relation to the society as a whole.

In presenting the universal meaning, symbolic forms engender the very means of valuation within the context. In utilising this means, the novel adopts the characterization of symbolic forms in endowing value upon the objects, persons, events, and situations it describes in its narrative form. In this way, it loses its innocence to the power relations encoded in and transmitted via the instrumentality of the symbolic forms. The novel becomes one among many other ways of creating and sustaining manipulating symbolic forms in the power play of positioning values and reproducing them. As for Foucault, I could then assert that the novel is an institutional mode of coding, distributing, and redistributing the existing power relations in society diffusely and ubiquitously. Within the redistributive power relations of power within the society, the novel assumes both the role of a privileged dominant genre and therefore a creator of combinations of relations of power as well as an instrument of the privileged, subservient in its function of transmitting encoded messages created by a dominant group to sustain and reproduce the existing relations of power. In its role as a handmaid of a dominant ideology, it seeks to sustain existing relations of power, whereas, in the other role as creator, it seeks to subvert or establish new relations of power. In attempting to play the creator within the dominant ideological structure, it adopts the posture of different combinations of power arrangement than the conventional or stereotyped ones. It, so to speak, observes and examines the same themes in different lights to bestow them with different values or a multiplicity of values hitherto absent to it. Operation within the same system, yet more diversified and complexified in valuation, represents its focus. In this sense, it creates and recreates itself in differentiation and combination. It can be characteristic of the structuralist model of the novel. However, in another role, in which the novel assumes a creative role, free from the dominant ideological mould, it seeks other bases of valuation that are not the dominant ideology but in other ideologies submerged by the dominant one. In so doing, the novel becomes subversive of the existing relations of power and projects what Lukacs, and later Goldmann, represent as potential consciousness. It is a characteristic attributable to deconstruction and the post-modernist novel. Moreover, the phenomenon may occur because of the conjunction of new circumstances needing new explanations and meanings and new social forces, such as the emergence of the new middle class in the post-modernist era, with its own vision and aspirations. This trend is also well-illustrated by the development of different visions through the centuries. In the pre-industrial period, religious and magical beliefs and practices were the dominating structuring forces of consciousness and meaning within any space and time framework. These informed as well as shaped the nature of literary work. The development of industrial capitalism eclipsed its antecedent by secularisation, with an emphasis and orientation towards economic activity and the rationalisation of social life (e.g., Marx's Communist Manifesto and Weber's Protestant Ethic). This orientation created new dimensions and possibilities for consciousness, especially in the sphere of political action, and the 'practical' assumes an ascendant role within consciousness. Social life, economics, and politics were thereby shaped from this position by the underlying structural ideas which are distinctly rational and empirical without any references to religion. The position of the subject is also affected and determined by this new structure. An emphasis on the objectives rather than the subjective, and the collective rather than the individual or vice versa is positioned in accordance with the ideological orientation. This is backed by those who control the means and resources of production, or by other dominant social forces which succeed in obtaining political power and hegemony. Under these consciousnesses, the structuration of life whole, culture, and language is much more of a practical, radical, and socio-political nature. Conflict is generated from this perspective as a powerful symbolic value, directed towards control, especially control of the means of production and political power. The symbolic forms of the dominant groups are counterposed by those of opposing forces, such as between the upper classes, the bourgeoisie, and the working class. The significance of these conflicts is usually renowned as revolutions. The novelist is positioned within one or the other of these categorisations, first of all, and within this social-historical reality of development. The symbolic forms they wield, the views they hold about the developments, and their valuations of them will inevitably derive from the realities and practicalities of this context, for they do not live outside it. Rather, they have been nurtured by this context and its internal atmosphere. In the post-industrial era, the tendency has been toward the containment of conflict by piecemeal reforms and pragmatic approaches. In another sense, the tendency is the realisation of the structural predeterminations constraining individual intention and action, yet the attempt is towards accommodating oneself into the structure while producing new realities within and from it. In another way, it can be from the point of view of the social, political, and economic structures as largely fixed yet invisible. However, space and time can still be manipulated in a flexible manner of arrangement within the existing dominating structure. Eclecticism is the most prominent feature of creative activity, and the rearrangement of time or space dominates the relations of power and productive activity and the production of new realities. What I have been discussing so far in the above illustrations is to establish that the novel has both an internal structure and existence dictated by and reflecting the internal composite and dynamics of its social-historical context, and on the other hand, an external ambiance monitored by the collective consciousness of the society in any particular time and space.

Consequently, in its internal forum, the novel reports events, describes persons and refers to places. These are objects or situations which will be familiar to the novelist because they derive their being from the existence of some such experiences within a historical context. Then readers understand them only because they have encountered similar experiences or recognise them in some form or other or because the structures and symbols employed by the dominant ideology and is universally employed. Nevertheless, the novelist, although constituted by the social-historical context is still capable of employing their faculties of imagination and intentionality.

They display this in the versatility and subtlety with which they make combinations of existing social forms to produce new realities and symbolic forms altogether. The novelist is consequently capable of multiplying symbolic forms through the arbitrary combination of existing ones – a new structuration process is underway. A new structuration process comes into being because although the novelist is utilising the conventional forms, each application comes into contact with a combination of events, persons and personalities, things, and situations.

It may seem in this sense that what I am trying to say is that the old order of things is given different perspectives by the novelist through their combination, application, and elaboration within other than the conventionalised contexts. In this sense, the novelist enlarges the possibilities which exist within the structure.

However, it must be noted that this enlargement of possibilities or realities does not constitute a transcendence of the structure itself within which the novelist exists and makes their production. What is achieved through this creativity is albeit a reproduction of the existing forms of signification in a more diversified form. What they achieve as diversity and new perspectives are still directed by the underlying principles shaping the structure of their contexts.

When ensues as diversity is actually a consequence of changes in position and rearrangements of time and space within the same structure.

Therefore, the transformation of the structure itself does not occur through the novel and its discourse; that is, the additional possibilities it creates by its combinations. On the contrary, its role turns out to be the reinforcement of the fundamental structure by its reflection and reproduction in multiplex forms, for its basic discourse is the discourse of this fundamental structure.

The serious implication of this role for the novel is that instead of being an instrument of transformation, it tends to make the existing structures it is reproducing rather invisible to the reader or consumer. This is how we might perceive Roland Barthes' approach in juxtaposing images, structurations of symbolic forms, and their repositioning away from their basic social, historical, and previous symbolic meanings to create entirely different contexts and interactions. There is another way, however, in which the novel may be of transformative value. That is, there is a different approach to the novel in its emphasis, which allows for suggesting and exploring structural alternatives and reforms rather than comprehensive structural reproductions. This approach shifts from an emphasis on the concentration on the internal structures of the grammatical construction of language and syntax (linguistics). Hence, it also shifts from the endorsement and adherence to the language of the controlling forces of a particular kind of novel to the comprehensive consideration of the novel as part of social consciousness.

This consciousness is regarded as consisting of a plurality of competing and conflicting ideologies, visions, or world views, hence of several possible alternatives or potential consciousnesses which could be actualised and evaluated (on the proviso that they could be brought to the status of the dominating ones within a socio-historical circumstance). Inevitably, this consideration lays an emphasis on the methodology of the novel and its fundamental controlling principle from which its structure derives –the world vision.

The significance of the approach is that ideology plays a central role in the writing and structuration of the novel, constituting its language or the nature and valuation of its discourse, the choice and combination of its symbolic forms.

To understand the novel, the reader needs to view it from both its internal structure and its external provenance regarding time and space (including the social, historical, positioning and arrangement, localisation, and personalisation). That means the methodological approach has implications for both the writing of the novel relating to its transformative value and for the reader in its understanding and interpretation.

The transformative value may derive from the fact that the novelist is an individual who consciously chooses a world vision among several existing possibilities, localises it into a particular context, and supplies it with a certain orientation or orientations and meanings. For the reader, these meanings and orientations can best be obtained by investigating the world vision of the novel with particular attention to the historical and social framework on which it was given flesh and the reasons why the author chose such locality, time, orientation, and positioning or arrangements or form for the narrative.

The same approach can lead us to understand why 'at different times, the same vision can assume different aspects; it can be revolutionary, sometimes defensive, reactionary and conservative, and sometimes even decadent.'[13]

So far in this chapter, I have been trying to establish how ideology plays a very important role in the formation and interpretation of the novel. As has already been noted, ideology has been neutralised and divested of its negative connotations in the mode cast by Napoleon Bonaparte and Karl Marx. I consider my use of ideology in application entirely in line with its acquired neutrality and equate it with such terms as 'world visions' (Goldmann), 'world view' (Sartre), and 'ideologemes' (Kristeva). These have profound implications for the writing of the novel, its characteristics, and its orientation, in the same way as they have profound implications for its interpretation.

I have been consciously abstract in many parts of this discussion. It is inevitable because I am essentially attempting to establish a hypothesis that ideology is at the very root of the novel, consequently, a methodology of interpretation of the novel. What I have been engaging in is considering the novel from its most important characteristic. I have established this characteristic as its ideological basis or grounding. In so doing, I have been influenced by many sociologists on ideology and cultural creation. Lucien Goldmann stands out as very perceptive in the analysis of the relationship of the novel to the rest of society and its consciousness (including the subject and the object relationships) while in very close alignment with my own perception of the whole project. He designs the methodology to examine the world vision of the novel and thus to perceive its meanings, dynamics, and characteristics based on the principles of explanation and interpretation, i.e., the novel's internal and external dimensions. I shall first bolster up this chapter on ideology and interpretation by examining Goldmann's methodology through the discussion of 'explanation' and 'description' before launching into a justification of the entire analysis through its concrete application to two of Elizabeth Gaskell's novels.

3| Lucien Goldmann and the Interaction of History and Social Structure in the Understanding of the Novel: A Methodological Development

Goldmann agrees with Merleau-Ponty that the novel reflects a certain social structure and history. In comprehending the novel, a valid criticism ought to take account of the realities of this reflection and its dialectic.

To illustrate how to understand and interpret the novel taking into account the issues as discussed in relation to history and social structure, Goldmann says:

To present a method as autonomous is positivism in the worst sense. We discuss method simply in so far as it is subordinated to the thing, to the necessity of comprehending facts, but in the debate with other ideologies, one must pose methodical problems in relation to our own way of understanding the facts. Description, the only scientifically valid description, is a comprehensive one. Description is interesting, valuable, and a viable instrument of research, only in so far as it enables us to understand.[1]

In this regard, Goldmann postulates a method of interpretation of the novel in dissociation from the positivistic approach of reification and from a descriptive approach that is unscientific and hardly capable of offering a comprehensive understanding of the world vision and 'truth content' of the novel: for example the purely biographical, psychological, philosophical, or intuitive approach which presupposes an abstract idea or first principles and works towards them. In a sense, then, these approaches lay down straight jackets into which the textual investigation and criticism are related only in its goodness of Fit; or rather, as with the intuitive approach, sympathies and affinities with the reader's experiences provide the ultimate criteria for the 'truth value' of the text.

What Godmann is postulating is that one can approach the novel in one of three ways:

- Textual analysis (positivistic)
- Intuitive methods, or by
- Dialectical methods

He regards the intuitive method as unscientific due to its heavy reliance on the incoherencies of sympathy and affinity with the reader or the critic's experiences. While the positivistic approach makes textual analysis its starting point, it does not ultimately hold together into any coherent pattern or system of understanding the text. For instance, the structuralist approach employs the text very heavily in its analysis of the novel.

However, the conclusions of its research emerge into incoherence as they are not endowed with meaning because the text itself is regarded as a self-contained system requiring no specific or possible meanings except those brought to it by the readers themselves through the juxtaposition of words, sounds, images, and events, based upon his own philosophical presuppositions.

The positivistic approach has its merits because it treats the text as a 'social fact.' This initiates its scientificity, giving it autonomy as an entity in itself, a reality worth studying for its own sake. Nevertheless, its danger lies in this very fact of its autonomy and isolation from the general reality from which it was generated in the first place. In treating the text in this manner, it is consequently reified, thus posturing it within the boundaries of conservatism and depriving it of dynamism and its possibilities. This very posture, according to Goldmann, deprives it of understanding. He explains that understanding the text can only be procured by considering the dialectical character of the text in relation to its significant global structures. The significant global structure of the novel genre is the universe created by the novel through its genesis from a certain set of values- what I have already discussed as ideology, world view, or world vision, such as the tragic vision in seventeenth-century literature typified in Racine's tragedies the significant global structure, as well as enabling the understanding between the text and the larger social and historical structure from which it was given birth.

For Godmann, this relationship is indispensable to any comprehensive apprehension of the novel, its universe, and its approximate true or real meaning and significance. Thus, in examining the writings of Mrs. Gaskell, for example, one ought to seek a comprehensive understanding of these writings and, thereby, their essence and significance by the analysis of the texts on the basis of the world view or the global structure of the nineteenth-century English society and class from which her thoughts took nurture and which have provided the skeleton around which she has shaped her writings whether in opposition to, collaboration with, or in alternative construction of a universe. Not only that, but the entire thought system of all of Mrs. Gaskell's novels, for example, can be consequently comprehended by the study of only one or two of her novels on the basis of the understanding of the fundamental set of values that inform and give significance to her writings and the structurations of word, image, sound, and events. This is because each novel in the collection of writings of the author constitutes a cell within the organic whole of the collection, and as Adorno will express it, each cell is a microcosm of the organic whole in as much as it is sustained by the fundamental set of values or world view that supports the organic whole.

What one is engaged in during criticism, understanding, or interpretation of the novel is the determination of the system or pattern that is discernible from the social-historical processes and their unintended consequences and the dialectic that is generated thereby. Like Weber and Merleau-Ponty, Goldmann believes that human history and its social processes do not follow strictly serially logical and identical phases. History is made and structured by the subjects out of the capital of events and objects at a particular moment, especially when the subjects treat a given historical situation as an object.

The structuration undertaken by subjects at any particular moment is the result of the unintended consequences or unexpected by-products of a previous structuration and its processes which create a crisis. A previous structuration turns up freak situations that need to be responded to. The response is made in adaptation to these situations. Consequently, these freak situations or unintended consequences become the new objects of structuration processes. These, in turn, produce new consequences and possibilities of which a choice is made for another set of structurations to begin. Thus, a dialectic is built upon a choice of possibilities, suggesting, too, what I have already noted from Godmann that human history and social processes do not proceed in a predetermined logical series.

The outcome of such a conclusion is that the picture emerges of a condition whereby subjects themselves provide constructs for the structurations-the world vision. This also means that no single world vision runs through the whole of human history like a lifewire. Instead, each turn of events, depending on what choice of possibilities are made in the structuration of unintended consequences, is shaped by an alternative world vision. Hence, one can speak, for example, of the sixteenth-century world vision of the chain of being, the seventeenth-century tragic vision, the eighteenth-century enlightenment, and the nineteenth-century ideologies. In all these processes, the subjects convert history into an object they can manipulate. The novelist captures the whole of this reality and its ramifications, objectifying it and thereby representing it in text.

I have already noted that the novelist is a product of the reality they are attempting to capture or recreate through the text. In the text of creation, they are, like the collective subjects, structuring the unintended consequences and possibilities, both the subject and the object. In this task, they are situating events and images within a particular view and moment, but then, they are themselves situated within it.

The novelist and the universe they create is consequently a moment within the larger reality it is representing, and what they represent is a product not of themselves but of the collective reality.

This is how Godmann perceives the novelist -as essentially part of the whole, saying that:

"I thus maintain that the ideas and work of an author cannot be understood as long as we remain on the level of what he wrote, or even of what he read and what influenced him. Ideas are only a partial aspect of a less abstract reality: that of the whole living man. And in his turn, this man is only an element in a whole made up of the social group to which he belongs. An idea he expresses or a book he writes can acquire their real meaning for us and can be fully understood only when they are seen as integral parts of his life and mode of behaviour. Moreover, it often happens that the mode of behaviour which enables us to understand a particular work is not that of the author himself but that of a whole social group, and when the work with which we are concerned is of particular importance, this behaviour is that of a whole social class." [2]

It would not be out of place to clarify Goldmann's position further by reference to a slightly longer quotation from Merleau ponty.

Maurice Merleau-Ponty observes the same relationship between the author as an individual and as such a part of the collective whole or the 'social' in the same likeness as Goldmann to say that:

> *...Certainly, nothing can change the fact our knowledge is partial in both senses of the word. It will never be confused with the historical- in-itself. We can never refer to completed totality, to universal history, as if we were not within it, as if it were spread out in front of us. The totality of which Lukacs speaks is, in his own terms, 'the totality of observed facts,' not of all possible and actual beings but of our coherent arrangement of all known facts. When the subject recognises himself in history and history in himself, he does not dominate the whole, as the Hegelian philosopher does, but at least, he is engaged in a work of totalisation. He knows that no historical fact will ever have its whole meaning for us unless it has been linked to all the facts we were able to know, unless it has been referred to as a particular*

moment in a single enterprise that unites them unless it has been placed in a vertical history which is the record of attempts with a meaning of their implications and of their conceivable continuations.[3]

The coherent arrangement of all known facts is precisely what the readers seek to discern as they seek an explanation of the text through interpretation or criticism. In examining the novels of Elizabeth Gaskell subsequently, this coherent structure or arrangement ought to be my preoccupation in the light of Goldmann's assertions; that is, the arrangement which informs the totality of the texts with meaning around a sustaining world view. Thus, my explanation will proceed in the realisation of DESCRIPTION of the text in its dialectical relationship, with the social in the manner Merleau-Ponty postulates so lucidly in alignment with Goldmann that:

> *There is only one knowledge, which is the knowledge of our world in a state of becoming, and this becoming embraces knowledge itself. But it is the knowledge that teaches us this. Thus, there is in that moment in which knowledge looks back on its origins, recaptures its own genesis, equals as knowing what it was as an event, gathers itself together in order to totalise itself, and tends towards consciousness. The same whole is, in the first relationship, history; in the second, philosophy. History is philosophy realised, as philosophy is history formalised, reduced to its internal articulations, to its intelligible structure.*[4]

Thus, it is realised in Goldmann's viewpoint that the degree of coherence which the novelist represents in the state of becoming is attributable to the social. It is manifested in its fundamental elements as a world vision (mainly comprising psychical and philosophical dimensions), in its state of becoming a social action and praxis, and in its development and expression in all their consequences.

What this means, in fact, is that what this coherence represents from the author's point of view in relation to society is that their consciousness derives from the non-conscious social categories, which the author transposes as an individual in the organisation of their universe instead of the content. These non-conscious categories are referred to by Goldmann as genetic structures because of their psychic genesis and structuration in the social and collective consciousness. The coherence the author achieves can all consequently be referred to as the organisation of these genetic structurations. The transposition of these genetic structures is made in relation to the definition of relationships between subjects, between subjects and objects, and subjects and nature without regard to content but to meaning.

Goldmann regards the specific or most distinct constitutive social phenomenon as the collective consciousness represented in class. Class is the most important group to which the individual belongs, at least from the standpoint of intellectual and artistic creation. That is how I would understand the assertion in 'Towards a Sociology of the Novel,' that every time it was a question of finding the infrastructure of a philosopher, a literary or artistic current, ultimately, we have been forced to consider, not a generation, nation or church, not a profession or any other social grouping, but a social class and its relations to society.[5]

The genetic structures are, therefore, attributable to the social constructs from this class composition and its assorted social components, which comprise it as a substantial entity.

From this standpoint, it is appropriate to make reference to the intersubjective or transindividual status of the author and the subsequent relation this bears to the coherence of the text, its interpretation, and its explanation. Precisely from this angle, Goldmann differs from linguistic structuralism. In describing this distinction in his 'Method in the Sociology of Literature,' he distances himself from the position of such structuralists as Althusser and Greimas, who posit the creativity factor to structures alone, hence denying men any role in historical transformations. Instead, he postulates genetic structuralism as a factor under which man is still the historical subject, possessing a creative role through human thought, emotions, and actions. Moreover, from this position, intersubjectivity derives its importance firstly as a partial function of the whole and secondly as an individual component acting in relation to other individuals.

By this position, taking one element of the whole, for instance, which is language, he asserts that it is not, as Todorov, for example, says, language that creates human beings but that human beings create language and employ it in the deployment of privilege.

In the deployment of privilege, the creation and structuration of behaviour and action in relation to others or to nature, which shape the historical dimension of the social, and individuals, act in concrete with one another within a stratum of the division of labour to tackle an object. Individuals thus act in relation to one another, not as object to object, but as subject to subject. The continuum of such relationship is what establishes the transindividuality of the subjects, otherwise referred to as the 'social' or the collective subject. On account of this, any examination of human facts by a subject is also the examination of its own reflection within the collectivity or the social.

What this postulation of the transindividual subject does for the explanation and interpretation of the novel is that it demotes the status of the individual author as a sense of single creative factor, ex nihilo, to the status of a 'midwife' of the collective consciousness.

Hence in the interpretation and explanation of the novel, Goldmann eschews the psychoanalytic and individualistic approach contained in the analysis of the text by the biography of the author and the influences upon them in themselves. Instead, he advocates the approach which analyses the text in relation to the collective subject and in which the real question can be formulated in such a way as why particular writers, philosophers, or novelists sustained precisely these influences in this particular period of their history or their life.

This raises the question of the collective subject in relation to particular periods or moments in the understanding of the novel. But firstly, I shall make a reference to the difference between Sartre's approach to understanding the text typified by psychoanalytical and individualistic approach in comparison to Goldmann's genetic structuralism in their references to the text of Genet, as a concrete example of what I have been saying so far and to render my position a little clearer.

Jane Routh notes that Sartre places considerable stress on the writer's self-awareness and social experience leading to:

- A psychoanalytical interpretation of the writer's internal experience, and

- A sociological analysis of the historical conditioning of literary meaning

In this experience, the two moments converge in a dialectic mode. In this dialectic, certain specific significances can be identified that link the writer's experiences to their class structure. It is these specific 'significatories' which are examined in detail, such as family, community, and work relations. Hence, Sartre, for example, finds what is particular to Flaubert in his writings and the specific significant thread on which his writing depends as his response to his family situation. Moreover, in examining Genet, he reconstructs his biography in a form that makes it illustrate a way of living contradictions in the social world. And this, in turn, rests on Sartre's identification of the root of Genet's writings as the connection between the family situation of orphanage or adoption as a response to the social world. Goldmann's view, as I have been outlining so far, repudiates the preponderance of the consciousness of human agency, and hence of the individual in responses to the social world, attributing it to be a collective subject because human agency derives its pattern ultimately from the structure which lies in the non-conscious corresponding to a level below the consciousness of the subject.

Goldmann, thus, understands the same works of Genet, more notably in the mode of collective consciousness. Hence, his understanding of Genet 'is as representative' of a left-wing intellectual group that experiences contradictions in the social world as a group. Sartre explains Genet's writings as a personal a way of resolving the stress to which society subjected him and of revenging himself on it. Individual projects, whether at a social or literary level, do not exist in Goldmann's work: Genet's work was neither discussed as an attempt to resolve individual social contradictions nor as an attempt to break, change or develop existing dramatic and literary conventions.'[6]

The understanding Goldmann accords his apparent lack of transformative character in the novel at the period in time is interesting. It must be noted that he has always considered the novel as an instrument rich with possibilities of transformative choices.

However, he also acknowledged the dangers of options open toward reification and conservatism. The late nineteenth century and the twentieth century seem to stand out for him as a period when this danger was clearly demolished owing to the domination of the market society. In 'Towards a Sociology of the novel,' he notes that the fetishisation of commercial goods has stifled the ability of collective consciousness to become actively engaged in the appreciation of its own historical reality. Instead, collective consciousness has stalled in becoming the infrastructure for reflecting economic life, effectively eliminating the operation of all other possibilities.

With the domination of the collective consciousness by economic life goes the implication that social life and all other possibilities are not dominated by the real use-value of life, goods, and services but by exchange value. Exchange value becomes an end in itself, effecting problems everywhere throughout society and setting up widespread discontent between society and the individuals within it. A problematic individual emerges from here.

This is where Goldmann invests the novelist with a high moral ground – the discovery of alternative possibilities to exchange values, hence the novelist is engaged in a 'search for values' apparently in this epoch against the dominating exchange values as a consequence of the crises it has generated among individuals.

The novelist, therefore, takes their foundation from the widespread discontent of individuals, conceptualises it, represents it, and invests its new universe with the responses of alternative quality values in the agreement of a transformative process. Thus, the novel form at this period usually contains at its centre the representative problematic individual experiencing quality values and also the constraints of society upon their individuality – as it were, a tension between the individual and society.

With this perception of understanding the novel, I shall launch into the discussion of Mrs. Gaskell's novels*: Mary Barton* and *North and South* with the hope of ascertaining a coherent structure in her examination of possibilities and transformative potential in the light of the problematic hero.

4 | Mrs. Gaskell's Novels

That a perfect understanding, and complete confidence and love, might exist between masters and men; that the truth might be recognised that the interests of one were the interests of all, and as such, required the consideration and deliberation of all; that hence it was most desirable to have educated workers, capable of judging, not mere machines of ignorant men; and affection, not by mere money bargains alone...

Many of the improvements now in practice in the system of employment in Manchester owe their origin to short earnest sentences spoken by Mr. Carson. Many and many yet to be carried into execution, take their birth from that stern, thoughtful mind, which submitted to be taught by suffering. [1]

In this concluding passage of *Mary Barton*, Mrs. Gaskell sums up the consequences of the problems spawned and hatched in the relationship between manufacturers and workers of Manchester in the mid-nineteenth century. In *North and South*, the same subject echoes in the tensions between manufacturers and the union. These were components of the interaction of capital, technology, foreign competition, untrained workers, and unions in nineteenth-century Britain, creating a situation of the 'self against the other.' The problem of the definition of the self in relationship to the objects and persons operant in the experience of the times emerged forcefully through an increasingly liberal economic and market system and scientific perception of man, which was rapidly taking over from a religious and family-oriented perception of man characteristic of the Pre-capitalist period. A new man was emerging – the economic and scientific man to replace the religious and aristocratic man.

Pre-capitalist and aristocratic society had depended on the support of mercantilism which had dominated European economic thought in the seventeenth and eighteenth centuries. Under the heterogeneous ideas of mercantilism, wealth and power were connected. Wealth was supposed to work in the service of power. To increase wealth is, thus, to increase power. Conversely, the possession of power means the accumulation of wealth. The acquisition of power was, nonetheless, threatened by the fact that it was limited. Wealth was considered in a typically reductionist and reified framework. There was only so much of it in the world in terms of precious metals, gold, and silver. Consequently, wealth and power flowed asymmetrically; that is, when one country gained by means of acquiring a stock of wealth, the other country from which it was gained lost. Trade was thus not a means of benefiting trading partners but one of taking as much as possible of the wealth of one state by another for the power associated with it. The means of acquisition are military expeditions or diplomatic leverage. On the other hand, the means of protecting the wealth acquired is by the imposition of taxation and trade blockades.

So far from the above factors, it is already apparent from Smelser's representation of mercantilism that the means of acquiring wealth or power is beyond any particular individual or group of individuals.

The state is thence the most logical owner and generator of wealth. To stimulate economic growth and increase the amount of wealth, the state has to employ its power to regulate the operations of industry and trade.

In this mercantilist view of economics and politics, the state has a monopoly over the operations of power and wealth and creates stability through the harmony between the two spheres. This is reflected in other spheres of life, which gain stability owing to their location within the stability of the states' monopoly of power and wealth. These were the spheres in which the individual bore relation to the state and assumed relevance. The individual could, thus, recognise and identify themselves by reference to aristocratic origins, religious position, or through educational representation, acquire a status of relevance to the state within an aristocratic or religious placement. This means, too, that the individual could not define themselves directly in relation to wealth and power except in relation to morality and reason.

In the nineteenth century, this conception and structure began to crumble. Economics gained a new concept through Adam Smith. Adam Smith challenged the mercantilist reductionism of wealth and its asymmetrical beneficence. In his *Wealth of Nations*, he contended that the wealth of nations is located in its protective base. That means the wealth of nations is based on its power to produce 'the necessities, comforts, and conveniences of life.'2 Money constitutes only the medium of exchange to enable the allocation of goods and services. Besides, the level of production is contingent on the division of labour, which in turn yields its highest according to how highly specialised it becomes. However, levels of high specialisation could be gained only on two counts - the size of the markets and the availability of capital.

Here, the attention is drawn to, and an emphasis is placed on the development of the widest possible markets to effect the distribution of the products of labour. An increase in wealth thereby comes through an expansion of international trade. Contrary to the mercantilist view, expansion could be achieved only through the liberalisation of trade. Moreover, wealth could not be increased through government monopolies and tariff restrictions or by direct political action. Governments should, therefore, keep out of economic decision-making for the custody of the economic agents. In this sense, Adam Smith advocates the redistribution of power within society and stricter differentiation between political and economic power. This concept in practice was known as 'Lassez-faire.'.

In Smith's conception, the only sphere of economic action in which the state or political power can relate is in the provision of a moral, legal, and institutional context within which business operations could effectively take place. It should, thus, be able to free itself from allocating any particular kind of favour to specific groups and enact laws to guarantee that sales and contracts are duly honoured. This proposal was in answer to the foreseen problem that could beset the concept from the exhibition of unbridled self-interest by businessmen, to offer an inbuilt control that could serve to stem the unbridled behaviour of business practice and utilisation of power. Hence, already the problems that could arise from the laissez-faire economic concept were very apparent.

Nevertheless, the most significant feature of this conception is the decentralisation of power from the state to economic agents. It now means that individuals and groups could establish their own wealth and relations of wealth to power and other advantages.

This individual wields practically enormous power and could define themselves in relation and reference solely to their wealth and the power obtained through such wealth. In the same way, they could define their relationship with other people and present their identity in reference to their economic power. The question is whether the individual will achieve recognition and self-fulfilment through such an identity or whether they will need different or additional frameworks within which to seek the achievement of self-recognition and fulfilment.

Fundamentally, these are questions at the root of Mrs. Gaskell's novels. In *Mary Barton*, the entrepreneurial spirit is represented by Mr. Carson and Mr. Thorton in *North and South*. Smith's conception produced, in general, new structures within which 'man' could define himself – 'economic man.' The effects were numerous both in terms of the individual and for society at large. In the society, Smelser argues that due to the new economic individual, rapid individual upward mobility in terms of wealth began to establish a new class of people - the *nouveau riche*. In attitudes and outlook, they were different from the aristocratic class of the pre-capitalist society and yet in wealth, comparable, although less educated. It is a situation clearly illustrated in the interaction between Mr. Hale and his family and Mr. Thorton and his colleagues.

The belief spawned by the rise of this new class was that anyone enterprising enough could become wealthy. Thus, Thorton gives the background story of his wretched past, his mother's enterprising spirit, 'being a woman of strong power, and strong resolve'[3], and his own, which first of all led him out of debt, bequeathed him by his father and from thence into his own entrepreneurship as a manufacturer and a wealthy man. The business acumen was amply represented in Thorton and was described in a passage:

There was a slight demand for finished goods, and as it affected his branch of the trade, he took advantage of it and drove hard bargains. He was sharp to the hour at the meeting of his strong sense and his power to see consequences at a glance and so come to a rapid decision. Older men, men of long standing in the town, men of far greater wealth - realised and turned into land, while his was all floating capital, engaged in his trade -looked to him for prompt, ready wisdom.[4]

Thorton himself, in reply to Mr. Hale's question on the nature of the relationship between the class of manufacturers and that of the workers, referred to the absolute possibility of the upward mobility of every individual through the operation of the market system and a sense of duty saying,

It is one of the great beauties of our system that a working man may raise himself into the power and position of a master by his own exertions and behaviour; that, in fact, everyone who rules themselves to decency and sobriety of conduct, and attention to his duties, comes over to our ranks; it may not always be as a master, but as overlooker, a cashier, a bookkeeper, a clerk, one on the side of authority and order. [5] A new society is emerging, and so is a new man. With these notions, the concept of the relationship between master and servant, which prevailed in the aristocratic society, is radically transforming into one of master and worker based on a relationship of management.

With regards to the kind of man this new arrangement of relationship creates, it deviates from the aristocratic 'gentleman.' Aristocratic man achieved his recognition of self-definition in relation to values connected to his position within the state and values engendered in the relationships between two persons.

The new man, economic or industrial, appropriates different grounds and values in his self-definition and attainment of recognition. Thorton again relates this rather eloquently in discussing his concept of 'man' with Margaret. He said:

> *I take it that 'gentleman' is a term that only describes a person in relation to others, but when we speak of him as 'a man,' we consider him not merely with regard to his fellow-men, but in relation to himself, to life - to time to eternity. A castaway lonely as Robinson Crusoe – a prisoner immured in a dungeon for life - nay, even a saint in Patmos, has his endurance, his strength, and his faith best described by being spoken of as 'a man'.* [6]

Thorton's reference to Robinson Crusoe and the isolation of St. John the Divine on Patmos could describe the condition of the new economic man who is going to be intensely individualistic and isolated while cutting this image for himself through self-definition against standards of wealth. In this sense, the individual's perception and relationships are determined by the sense of his individualism and how much wealth the other outside himself can generate. The mode of valuation of the 'other' or things external to himself and the appreciation of his own individualism derive entirely from standards of wealth and market operations. Thus, Margaret, coming from the rural south, encountered the phenomenon for the first time, wondering about Thorton's sense of judgement which is entirely contrary to her more religious valuation of events and things. She remarked to her father:

Oh, Papa, by that, testing everything by the standard of wealth. When he spoke of the mechanical powers, he evidently looked upon them only as new ways of extending trade and making money. And the poor men around him - they were poor because they were vicious - out of the pale of his sympathies because they had not his iron nature and the capabilities that it gives him for being rich. [7]

The sustenance of wealth and consequently the realisation of self-definition, which has become inseparable from it, ought to be carried forward through the expansion of markets and the beating off of foreign competition, which constituted the greatest threat to the production of wealth and this important condition of the 'self' and its possession. Benjamin Ward effectively describes the viable conditions for this attainment in the 'Ideal world of economics.' He states that:

> *...the profit-seeking merchant needs freedom because his profits are not to be found in doing something different, in finding some opportunity neglected by others...And order is the environment within which markets serve their enabling functions most effectively, providing information and opportunity to the energetic seeker after profits and satisfying the desires of those with both wants and means.*[8]

Freedom for the entrepreneur, as Smith's conception, will have it has to be guaranteed by the state. On the other hand, if the freedom of the entrepreneur is to be productive, there must exist a complete or great degree of order both under the auspices of the state and by the discipline of the workplace among workers. The entrepreneur is hereby left with an unlimited scope of operation, which could translate as power - power over the marketplace, power over workers and consumers, and power autonomous of and in juxtaposition to the state. An enormous sense of self-worth and identity is thus invested in the manufacturer, which Thorton describes in answer to Mr. Hale's enquiry regarding manufacturers' objections to acts of parliament.

> *'Yes,' he said, 'I have, and many others have as well. And with justice, I think. The whole machinery now - of the cotton trade is so new that it is no wonder if it does not work well in every part all at once. Seventy years ago, what was it? And now, what is it not? Raw, crude materials came together; men of the same level, as regarded opportunities and probabilities, which distinguished some and made them far-seeing as to what great future lay concealed in that rude model of Sir Richard Arkwrightts.*[9] *The rapid development of what might be called a new trade gave those early masters enormous wealth and command. I don't mean merely over workmen; I mean over purchasers over the whole world's market. Why I may give you an instance, an advertisement inserted not fifty years ago in a Milton paper, that so - and - so (one of the half-dozen calico printers of the time) would close his warehouse at noon each day. Therefore, all purchasers must come before that hour. Fancy a man dictating in this manner the time when he would sell and when he would not sell ... we will hardly submit to the decision of an umpire, much less to the interference of a meddler with only a smattering of the knowledge of the real*

facts of the case, even though that meddler be called the High Court of Parliament. [10]

In addition to this, or rather more symbolic of the power of the manufacturer, are the power of science and technology and the 'magic' of its productive capabilities. The industrial revolution, which began with a series of inventions in the cotton industry, formed a basis for transforming the structure of human consciousness regarding power and productivity. Steam power and machinery were to transform the organisation and meaning of labour in relation to persons and commodities. In terms of power, machines were substituted for human skill, and energy replaced the animate sources.

In terms of advantage and productivity, machines were 'rapid, regular, precise and tireless.' [11]. This presaged for man a new and unlimited supply of power or energy. In regard to labour this abundant source of inanimate power was supposed to substitute for and hence ease the physical exertions and toil of human labour. Regarding productivity, it was privileged in the drastic limitation of time needed to produce commodities and the superiority in the number of goods capable of being produced within the same time limits compared to human power. The possibilities of cheaper commodities and new and wider markets were the expected outcomes of this novel generative process.

The sheer superiority of machines in comparison to man in productivity, capabilities, and unlimited and efficient functioning was amazing and Promethean, i.e., it was translated into a principle. The manufacturer owning the machinery wielded power over this enormous force and all its manipulations - he was the master of all. There is, in possessing the source of unlimited power over animate and inanimate things, he was a kind of deity. Thorton, in a fit of excitement over this amazing power and his self-identification with its supremacy, explained to Mr. Hale and Margaret about the operation of the machines and their power:

> *...so thoroughly was he occupied in explaining to Mr. Hale the magnificent power. Yet, the delicate adjustment of the might of the steam-hammer, which was recalling to Mr. Hale some of the wonderful stories of subservient genii in the Arabian nights one moment stretching from earth to sky and filling all the width of the horizon, at the next obediently compressed into a vase small enough to be borne in the hand of a child, And this imagination of power, this practical realisation of a gigantic thought, came out of one man's brain in our good town. That very man has it within him to mount, step by step, on each wonder he achieves to higher marvels still. And I'll be bound to say, we have many among us who, if he were gone, could spring into the breach and carry on the war which compels, and shall compel, all material power to yield to science.* [12]

The structure of consciousness has shifted from the limitations of power to the unlimitedness of power, comparable to Smith's thesis of the unlimitedness of wealth - the individual is in possession of an unlimited capacity for the production of wealth. The entrepreneur has thereby moved from the limitations of mundane materials and the physical world to a metaphysical representation of himself in the principle of power. His language and structuring of relationship with things and persons are consequently being moulded in this grid of power. It is not difficult to perceive then why Thorton could be cast in his impassive and defiant pose against the workers' strike and on the platform in front of his factory. Margaret, who remains outside this category of manufacturers despite her association with the Thorton, perceives differently, wishing for a different kind of response from the entrepreneur.

Thorton's sense of power and the consciousness of himself as the principle of power conduct him to a politics of 'no compromise' with his workers. It must be remembered, though, that this is a sound principle in strictly logical conformity with the free market principles and productivity. If new markets are to be opened, wealth to be created, and foreign competition to be beaten off, then goods have to be produced cheaply and rapidly. If this is to be achieved accordingly and efficiently, it requires all resources to be employed to their maximum limits and the due requirements adopted.

Nevertheless, the principle concentrates solely on the relations between things and completely cuts out the relation between persons. Already I have cited Thorton's structure of consciousness with regard to his self-definition elaborated in the concept of 'man' as in relation only to time, place, and eternity, with persons excluded.

No wonder in examining Thorton's perception, we enter the manufacturer's world, the things which constitute his basis of valuation and symbolisation of relations and, thereby, of life as a whole.

In this case, it is the labour process and the instruments of productivity and hence of power. The instruments of productivity and power must be protected by all means. Any disagreement, deviation, or disaffection towards this process must thus be perceived as a threat to the manufacturer's perception of himself and his potency. The most obvious manner to protect it is to exhibit its full force and rigour by assuming a position of resolve and 'no compromise.'

A position of 'no compromise' here was manifested in three ways:

- To insist on the principles of the free market,
- To acquire an alternative labour force,
- To reject the requests for wage increases in a test of wills

Besides politics, the realisation, too, obtains that the entrepreneur's criteria for the valuation of all other aspects of life have been altered by his self-definition as a 'man.' His sense of morality, religion, education, and society has all been transformed from the pre-capitalist mode into a principled, impassive, and individualistic mode. It is cast in the mould of machine - efficiency, legitimated by results, eternalised by theory, and objectified in its representatives.

To gain a comprehensive view of the entrepreneurial outlook, then, it would be very important for the enquirer to realise the inseparability of the machine from the entrepreneur and to give prominence to the discussion of the nature and characteristics of the instruments of productivity rather than the relations between entrepreneurs and workers. Mrs. Gaskell's construction of the narrative of *North and South* is consequently structured to give prominence to the perception of the manufacturer. Thorton gains prominence on the narrative stage by probing his attitudes, motives, nature, and perception. This is explored through the encounter with Margaret and the Hale family, and these perceptions, attitudes, motives, and nature we could identify within the framework of the theory of laissez-faire economics, a theory that guarantees unlimited power which proffers extreme possibilities in practice, and in another, become divorced completely from humanity and humaneness if carried to its logical conclusions.

Mrs. Gaskell seems to steer towards the crises which are the by-products of these processes and demonstrates in her novels that these have consequences not only for the entrepreneur but induces for their counterparts who are dominated, the workers, both severe physical and moral crises. It is so depicted in *North and South* in the conditions and attitudes of the workers but is given more prominence in *Mary Barton*, where the novelist examines the individual's self-recognition or non-recognition under the changing world view and its processes, particularly through John Barton and his moral dilemma.

The absolute power of the entrepreneur in terms of ownership of machinery and production processes constitutes the motor for a radically transforming society in its valuation and its ancillary institutions, such as the family and religion. Technology and science and the power they engendered tended to undermine the stability of family and religion, questioning how natural they were to human existence and self-definition and thereby raising the crises in the individual about self-definition and the meaning of his existence.

This was bound to affect mostly the workers and those not belonging to the entrepreneurial category. This is because, as we have already been trying to explore, the entrepreneur is clear in his mind with respect to the criteria of his self-recognition and definition. It has been established in technology and economic theory. The non-entrepreneur, on the other hand, is yet to establish their own criteria of self-recognition and definition, which has been displaced and superimposed by the former, in obvious supremacy over it. Secondly, in the new relationships constructed out of the world view of the entrepreneur, the human labour was calculated as merely a part of the machinery of productivity. Thus, whereas the entrepreneur was conscious of his self and its source of the definition, the worker had yet to grasp the logic of this new world view which related to persons as simply one among many other things or as 'things-for-others,' not 'persons -for- themselves.'

The basis for meaning for the self for the worker has been dislocated and decentred from family and religion to the collective signification as 'labour' and 'the other' by the entrepreneur. It is obvious to perceive, therefore, how so much the machine and its characteristics have been the centre of these processes and of the entire restructuring of consciousness.

In the case of the worker as an individual, he was liable to undertake his duties under gigantic and powerful machinery which dwarfed him, such as in cotton and woolen factories. His powerlessness could not be more pronounced and symbolised. Moreover, despite the power of these machines, the man was still the operator, often handling the machinery in its motions or in finishing off and polishing the products of these machines to their final perfection or performing the strategic operations by hand. In the metallurgy factories, for instance, the process is described in a letter by Lady Bell saying:

> *From the moment when the ironstone is lifted off the trucks, then dropped into the kilns, afterward taken to the furnace, and then drawn out of it, it has not been handled by any*

other means than the arms of powerful men, whose strength and vigilance are constantly strained almost to breaking point. [13]

Thus, an enormous amount of power, both physical and mental, in concentration was exacted in the operation of these machines. The weakening of the individual and his position in relation to these objects is nonetheless eloquently represented in such connections.

Another mode by which power was extracted from the individual by machinery, albeit indirectly, was in the relations of person-to-person with respect to the machines, in this case, specifically to entrepreneurs. Machines have created the opportunity for the substitution of workers. They enabled entrepreneurs to create a large pool of reserve workers who could be employed as bargaining chips against disgruntled workers, thus rendering the individual powerless even vis–a–vis human relationships. The superabundance of labour further occasioned entrepreneurs to engage in capital-saving rather than the risk of labour-saving investments. Consequently, even where machines could replace human toil, they were not given priority. It was cheaper and more controllable to employ human skills, in some cases because their performance against machine products was better and in other cases because of consumers' preference for hand-made goods.

The whole ambiance of the worker's relationship between 'self' and 'thing' and 'self' and 'person' was constructed around machinery and power. No wonder the powerlessness which affected the individual in relation to these 'others' generated a dislike for machinery and its symbolic representatives, the manufacturers. In one sense, the individual has to define themselves within these limitations of powerlessness within which their whole experience is confined. Autobiography and biography present the best possible means of translating these processes in terms of the individual experience of work and the world of power and powerlessness to view and articulation. This also suggests the form of Mrs. Gaskell's novels in their realistic and reflectionist narrative. Nonetheless, they are reflectionists, not in the sense of carbon-copied historical narratives, but in the sense of the practical, theoretical, and emotive structuring and articulation of the experience of the individual in relation to their instruments of production and the entrepreneur on the other hand from their position of perception - i.e., of the individual as a worker, and the individual as an entrepreneur.

The challenge for the individual as a worker developed out of the crisis generated through the realisation that old categories of self-definition through the family and religion are no longer adequate or even applicable in relation to making meaning of their life and work. Now, work is not necessarily engaged in feeding or improving the family's condition or as a religious duty to God. The emphasis has shifted to the engagement in work as a duty to produce and productivity, and no other category has assumed propriety of the obligation for work. Inevitably, the worker as part of the machinery for production has been commodified.

This is made more poignant by the fact that the need was not felt for the worker's education to understand, make meaning of, and take control of his world of work and its processes as the entrepreneur has managed to position himself. Thus, in the aftermath of the workers' strike, in an argument with Mr. Higgins, he pointed out the cause of the differences in the different positions they occupy and the different perceptions of truth that could be occasioned by the attempt to make meaning from the self's experience of the world around and inside itself:

> *... it might, it might not. There are two opinions that go to settle that point. But suppose it was truth double strong, it were no truth to me if I couldna take it in. I dare say there's truth in your Latin book on your shelves: but it's gibberish and not true to me unless I know the meaning o' the words. If yo', sir, or any other knowledgeable, patient man come to me and says he'll teach me what the words mean and not blow me up if I'm a bit stupid or forget how one thing hangs on another - why, in time I get to see the truth of it, or I may note I'll not be bound to say I shall end in thinking the same as any man. And I'm not one who think truth can be shaped out in words, all neat and clean, as th'men at th' foundry cut out sheet-iron. Some bones won't go down with everyone. It'll stick here i' this man's throat, and theri't'other's. Let alone that, when down, it may be too strong for this one, too weak for that. Folk who sets up to doctor th'world ei 'their truth, mun suit different for different minds; and be a bit tender in th'way of giving it too, or th'poor sick fools may spit it out i' their faces.* [14]

Here Higgins offers a vivid illustration of the possibilities of different 'truths' generated from different practical experiences of things and the articulation of the different data. The possibility of communication of some 'truth' from some particular position requires a relationship of understanding between the subject and the 'other.'

Apparently, the lack of understanding or yet of the will to understand congeals persons into parallel positions and creates self-definitions and languages which are irreconcilable with one another, which do not have to be necessarily so. Thus, for example, while entrepreneurs regarded productivity as labour, workers regarded it as toil both from their different premises and articulation of experiences of power and productivity. In the case of Gaskell's world of entrepreneurs and workers, this actually conducts to a politics of resolve and no compromise on either side to incarnate a strike and all its consequences. In assessment, 'the workmen's calculations were based (like too many of their masters) on false premises. They reckoned on their fellow men as if they possessed the calculable powers of machines, no more, no less...' [15]

In *Mary Barton*, where Gaskell narrates matters much more from the position of the worker's self-perception and moral crises, John Barton is representative of the dislodged individual who has yet to rediscover a lost self in self-definition in the light of the transforming world of power and its entirely different relationship structure.

The nature and effects of powerlessness were piercingly dramatised in the life of John Barton, who was reduced from a confident, self-assured family head and respectable leader of a community of workers to a physical and moral wretch in the end. John Barton's hopes were still pegged to the powers of the state to intervene in rescuing the worker from his powerlessness through an act of parliament. He failed. The realisation that the state was as distant from the worker and that the individual was no more than a non-entity in the crowd broke upon him on his delegated mission to represent the workers of Manchester in arguing his case in London.

He had only occasion to catch a glimpse of the cavalcade of royalty. For the rest, he was not even noticed as a delegate - sneered at by the police, and his voice drowned in the tussling crowd. The sense of powerlessness was deepened by the experience, which effectively projected the fact that the individual was on his own isolated. The self had to come to terms with its isolation and powerlessness in relation to both entrepreneur and the state.

Since there was no prospect of the state intervening to restore some measure of power to the individual, the individual seeks an alternative source of power, finding it in the collectivity: in a union of individuals afflicted by the same powerlessness, strength, and power could be produced to contend the power of entrepreneurs, and to restore a sense of empowerment. Hence, Barton and Boucher felt enthusiastic for union activities in *North and South*. Against this background, he finds a source of self-definition and grounding.

Again, unlike the entrepreneur whose articulation of power was couched in the impersonal machines of production and the demands of the markets, those of the workers were articulated in the intelligence and passion of human relationships and interaction.

Hence two entirely different attitudes and approaches to the resolution of issues emerge, which are antagonistic to each other. The two approaches merge in resemblance only in their uncompromising postures.

The novels argue from many references that in both postures, a measure of truth could be found. Nonetheless, the truth of both postures was lost in extremism. Thus, Carson argues with Job Legh and Wilson in the attempt to find a rationale for John Barton's behaviour in murdering his son, still insisting on justifying the position born out of the determinism of the market forces:

That's the notion all of you got. Now, how in the world can we help it? We cannot regulate the demand for labour. No man or set of men can do it. It depends on events that God alone can control. [16]

Thus, Carson justifies the attitude of the entrepreneur by an appeal to an inevitable power and principle incapable of being controlled by human beings except to submit to it - facts that are independent of human control. On the other hand, Job Legh, in defence of John Barton's sincere thoughts and acting as a proxy of his feeling, discounts the principle of inevitability in the principles of production and the markets, saying quite convincingly that:

> *You can never work facts as you would fix quantities and say, given two facts, the product is so and so. God has given men feelings and passions which cannot be worked into the problem because they are forever changing and uncertain. God has also made some weak; in body, another in mind, another in the steadiness of purpose, a fourth can't tell right from wrong, and so on...I ask your pardon, sir; I can't rightly explain the meaning that is in me. I'm like a tap that won't run but keeps letting it out drop-by-drop so that you have no notion of the force of what's within.* [17]

John Barton's tragedy developed because, as an individual, his articulation of the events and facts led him to understand that both religion and the family no longer provided the grounds for meaning and self-definition in a space increasingly coveted by machines and productivity. Religion and the family were themselves under serious transformation, and in the crisis of redefining themselves, they became destabilised, causing religious crises. Mr. Hale was profoundly affected, and his religious doubts and resignation as a minister were symptomatic of the shock engineered by the new rising power of science and technology. Barton's attempt is the search for alternatives that were, in any case, less powerful than the dominating world view, and yet if he did not, he could neither have empowered himself. In either case, he realised his condition but had no means of self-recognition and self-possession in the face of a more articulate and dominating, although not necessarily more truthful, world view. He failed because, cut off from his old basis of valuation, he no longer had a reference point for his values except in the emotion and humanism rooted in the old world view to which he unfortunately no longer had access either. A deep moral question and indeterminacy arise - What is 'good'? What is 'moral'? There are neither any ready-made answers nor any clear path to them.

Mrs. Gaskell seems to construct a path by pointing to other alternative possibilities of empowerment of both the entrepreneur and the worker-individual over the inanimate forces of the market and the union but conceives this empowerment in terms of cooperation or consensus an emphasis on the person-to-person relationships which could contain and control inanimate forces and harness them to the benefit of empowering both entrepreneur and worker. A new structure of management and worker relationships are under consideration - in political terms, a co-operative and democratic organisation of the workplace and decision-making which could determine a new basis for the definition of the self for both manufacturer and worker.

A very interesting aspect of Mrs. Gaskell's analysis is that she remains ambiguous so far as the resolution of contradictions is concerned. She has successfully charted the universe of the epoch in the universe of her novels and has come up with its contradictions, especially in the operation of the principles in the moral sphere, as depicted in the lives of the capitalists and the workers, represented in Thorton and Carson on the one hand, and John Barton and Boucher on the other.

She has noted the contradictions of both power and violence in both camps - the free market system and its representatives, the manufacturers on the one hand, and the humanists and its representatives, and the workers on the other.

Despite the contradictions, Mrs. Gaskell, in fact, does not condemn or eliminate either of these representations. Nevertheless, she is unable to offer any conclusive resolutions to the contradictions inherent in these processes, as far as her novels are concerned. Her tentative attempts at some resolution are not detailed and appear even more uncertain at the end of *North and South*.

At the end of *Mary Barton*, a resolution of the contradictions and conflicts by means of consensus between worker and manufacturer seemed very much within easy reach. Thus, Mr. Carson's 'short earnest sentences' were all that was needed for reforms to take place.

In *North and South*, on the other hand, Mr. Thorton realises the need for the human relationship as an essential factor in the operation of the free market. Nevertheless, he perceives its acute limitations too.

Again in *North and South,* the contradictions inherent in the sensitivity of the free market to fluctuations of fortune and failure of the manufacturer are highlighted in the vicissitude of Mr. Thorton. The contradictions Mrs. Gaskell highlighted and the attempts she made at their resolution can be represented as follows:

Worker

Mary Barton

- John Barton dies repentant of his violence in the murder of young Carson.
- Job Leng and Wilson hold discussions with Mr. Carson to outline their perception of the manufacturer.
- Mr. Carson orders reforms.

North and South

- Boucher commits suicide, unrepentant of his instigation of a violent strike.
- Higgins, a moderate, becomes a friend of Mr. Thorton.

Manufacturer

- Mr. Carson grieves over the murder of his son.
- Mr. Carson holds discussions with Job Legh, and Wilson is converted to a humanistic approach.
- Mr. Thorton denounces the violence of radical elements of the Union, such as Boucher.
- Mr. Thorton's factory collapses from the merciless uncertainty and fluctuations of the market and the damage done through the workers' strike.
- Mr. Thorton stands aside with profound humility to see his brother-in-law, Mr. Watson, shoot to fortune and admiration through daring speculation while his own fortunes crumble through faulty speculation.

North and South

- Mr. Thorton realises rather belatedly from friendship with Higgins that a manufacturer-worker relationship could be of great benefit to the manufacturing process and that "we have all of us one human heart."
- Thorton advocates actual personal contact between individuals of different classes as a means of bringing them together rather than by any institutional arrangements, no matter how expertly structured.
- Thorton advocates the interaction of individuals of different classes not because it can prevent strikes but because it can defuse strikes of the bitter form hitherto experienced.

Although Mrs. Gaskell offers no clearly defined resolutions to the conflict, she has been able to define the contradictions in a deeply penetrating fashion.

As Goldman posits, the great novelist is one who is able to identify and reconstruct the contradictions of their universe in the universe of the novel. This Mrs. Gaskell has thoroughly achieved.

Conclusion

In *Mary Barton* and *North and South*, I have identified the world view as economism, the laissez-faire proposition of Adam Smith, which shaped the discourse of the novels. Within this framework, a discourse has been formulated and manipulated in different ways to carry the experiences of the world of work and production in relation to the self and its definition, both by the worker as an individual and the entrepreneur as an individual. Mr. Carson and Mr. Thorton defined themselves in relation to the power conferred by machinery and the working of market forces. The meaning of events and attitudes towards these and other persons were, in turn, determined and shaped by the anchorage and the reference point. On the other hand, John Barton and Boucher were no longer clear about their anchorage through this reference point for making meaning of the overwhelming events which affected both physical well-being and self-worth. With the dominating economism in operation, which divorced the impersonal processes of work from humanism, they were left stranded in their continued integration of both spheres. However, as they realise, this continued integration or non-differentiation of spheres did not make meaning anymore in the face of the abolition of the self as the basis of making meaning. The search for meaning with the self leads to restlessness, which is pooled together in union membership and generates a sense of power to uphold the self in a bargain against a world that excludes it.

Ironically, the crusade for humanism degenerates into a passion for violence - in the case of John Barton, in the murder of Carson's son, and at the collective level, a new tyranny of vengeful strikes such as the one against Thorton, which the novelist described as 'the demoniac desire of some terrible wild beast for the food that is withheld from his ravening.' [1] Its tyranny against its own members was also revealed in its coercions as described by Higgins:

> *Well! If a man doesn't belong to th' union, them as works next looms has not to speak to him - if he's sorry or ill, it's a' the same; he's out of bounds; he's none of us; he comes among us, but he's none of us. It some places them's fined who speaks to him... must yo' try that, miss ten hours for three hundred days, and yo'll know a bit what th' union is.'*[2]

Nonetheless, unions are not intrinsically violent or disruptive to order which is the most compatible condition for productivity and its processes. Higgins commends it as well:

He'd show the world that th' real leaders of the strike were not such as Boucher, but already thoughtful men; good hands, good citizens, who were friendly to law and judgement and would uphold order; who only wanted their right wage, and wouldn't work, even though they starved, till they got 'em; but who ne'er injure property or life.[3]

Within this framework, the nature and utility of trade unions are discussed in the new order of productivity and divisions of power.

How relevant are trade unions and their values of humanism to productivity? Has man power over economic processes, or should man be trapped in the processes of economic determinism?

The murder carried out by Barton and the nature of the unions have opened a vista into what tyrannical forms the uncontrolled exercise of passions can generate within the power of the collectivity. It has the potential of trampling underfoot the very individual it has constituted itself to empower and to protect; and also of becoming an uncontrollable monster in the same way as the uncontrolled or unrestricted practice of the market forces and productivity constitutes a monster that tramples down and obliterates the individual by becoming reductionist and impersonal.

In *Mary Barton*, Gaskell examined the problem mainly from the worker's perspective. In *North and South*, she does so from the entrepreneur's perspective. On the other hand, from her articulation of the facts and events, she takes a position that perceives the possibility of achieving the interests of both parties through a politics of understanding, something that seems to come together in the meeting between Mr. Carson, the employer, and Job Legh and Wilson representing the deceased employee, John Barton. Recognition of the workers' situation did not come to Carson until, in seeking to come to terms with the loss of his son and its motivations, he had to engage in discussion and patient listening to the pains, thoughts, and emotions of the repentant murderer through his friends Legh and Wilson. The meeting served as an eye-opener to him on the condition of the labourer as a human and set him on a different definition of his relationship with the object and persons. Consequently, a crisis had occasioned a redefinition of events and restructuring of the relationship with the object and persons. Consequently, a crisis had occasioned a redefinition of events and the restructuring of relationships. This is echoed within Carson's attempts at reforms in his factory, rendering the possibility of a man constructing and controlling the processes of economism so that it does not become deterministic, turning man into the object rather than the subject.

In reaching the analysis, I have tried to establish that discourse is essential for the construction and interpretation of the novel. Discourse, however, is nothing static. It is dynamic in the sense that it manifests in many different forms and creates different possibilities. Moreover, it is not something that exists ex nihilo. It is created ultimately and socially.

The social construction of discourse depends on the dominating ideology existing within a time and space continuum and the possibilities of combination existing within and outside its own ambiance. This is usually generated by a crisis of one sort or another, opening up many different choices and combinations of ideas. The novel is the universe that brings together the dominating choice or ideology and its discourse in actual or possible combinations. When the novel steps outside this ideology or world view and offers alternative discourses, it becomes subversive and potentially transformative.

The circumscription by time and space makes discourse and its world view intelligible only within a dialectic and its possibilities. This has implications for the reader. The characteristic of time and space endows the world view with a quality of history. History is constituted into philosophy by restructuring events and their combinations around their constructing world view. The attempt to trace out a coherent structure in the historical constitution of a world view in the novel in relation to its structures and its constructs is, at the same time, interpretation and understanding. This is the methodology that has informed the analysis of the nature and interpretation of the novel.

Endnotes

Chapter One

1. Bernstein, B., Class, Codes and Control, Vol Ill, 2nd edition (London: Routledge and Regan Paul, 1975) p16.
2. Lavine, T.Z., From Socrates to Sartre: the philosophic guest (Toronto: Bantam Books, 1984) PI 94.
3. Nietzsche, F., Human, all too human (London: Penguin Books, 19S6) transl. R.J. Hollingdale, PI 1.
4. Hollingdale, R.J., transl. A Nietzsche Reader (London: Penguin Books, 1977) p69.
5. Routh, J et al. eds., The sociology of Literature (London: Wood Mitchel & co Ltd., 1977) p172.

Chapter Two

1. Thompson, J. B., Ideology and Modern Culture (London: Polity Press, 1990) p29.
2. Ibid, p29.
3. Ibid, p32.
4. Lavine, T. Z. Op cit. p208.
5. Ibid, p209.
6. Thompson, J.B. Op cit. p34.
7. Ibid, p35.
8. Arthur, C.J. ed., Karl Marx and Frederick Engels: selected works in one volume (London: Lawrence and Wishart, 1970) p41.
9. Thompson, J.B. Op cit. p41.
10. Ibid, p48.
11. Ibid, p53.

12. Goldmann, L., The Hidden God (London: Routledge and Kegan Paul, 1964) transl. Philip Thody, p19.
13. Ibid, p21.

Chapter Three

1. Goldmann, La, Cultural Creation in Modern Society (Oxford: Basil Blackwell, 1977) transl. Bart Grahl, p134.
2. Goldmann, L., The Hidden God (London: Routledge and Kegan Paul, 1964) transl. Philip Thody, p7.
3. Merleau-Ponty, M., Adventures of the Dialectic (London: Heinemann Educe, 1974) p32.
4. Ibid p32.
5. Goldmann, L., Towards a Sociology of the Novel (London: Tavistock Publications Ltd., 1964) transl. William Buelhower, p102.
6. Routh, J. et al., eds., The Sociology of Literature (London: Wood-Mitchel & co., 1977) p152.

Chapter Four

1. Gaskell, E., Mary Barton (Oxford: Oxford University Press, 1987) p457.
2. Smelser, N.J., The Sociology of Economic Life (Englewood Cliffs: Prentice-Hall Inc., 1976) 2nd edition, p6.
3. Gaskell, E., North, and South (Oxford: Oxford University Press. 1982) p212.
4. Ibid, p84.
5. Ibid, p164.
6. Ibid, p87.
7. Ward, B., The Ideal World of Economics (London: Macmillan, 1979) p336.

8. Arkwright (1732 92) improved the existing type of a powered spinning frame between 1767 and 1769 so that high-quality cotton thread could be produced of any desired fineness and hardness; this initiated the modern cotton industry.
9. Gaskell, E., North, and South (Oxford: 1982) p83.
10. Sarnuel, Re, 'Workshop of the World' in History Workshop Journal (Issue 3, Spring. 1917) p43
11. Gaskell, E., Op. Cit. p80.
12. Sarnuel, R., Op. Cit. p43.
13. Gaskell, E., Op. Cit. p230.
14. Ibid p228.
15. Gaskell, E., Mary Barton (Oxford: 1937) p453.
16. Ibid p454.
17. J.A. Banks, in his book, 'Prosperity and Parenthood,' notes that from the middle of the nineteenth century, the family began to be planned rationally and scientifically in response to Mathus' theories of population and its correlation to poverty and wealth. Marriage and the number of children in a family began to be rationally determined by occupation and income, especially by the middle class.

Conclusion

Gaskell. E., Mary Barton

1. (Oxford: 1987) p176.
2. Ibid, p 232.
3. Ibid, p 200.

Bibliography

1. Abrams, M.H., The Mirror and the Lamp (Oxford: Oxford University Press, 1977)
2. Adorno, Theodor, Aesthetic Theory (London: Routledge and Kegan Paul, 1984) transl. C. Lenhardt.
3. Althusser, C., Lenin and Philosophy and other essays (New Left Books, 1971)
4. Arthur, C.J. ed., Karl Marx and Frederick Engels: selected works in one volume (London: Lawrence and Wishart, 1970)
5. Banks, J.A., Property and Parenthood (London: Routledge and Kegan Paul, 1965)
6. Barthes, Roland, The Semiotic Challenge (Oxford: Basil Blackwell Ltd., 1988) transl. Richard Howard
7. Mythologies (London: Grafton Books, 19S9) transl. Annette Lavers
8. Barrett, Michelle, et al. (eds), Ideology and Cultural Production (London: Croorn Helm, 1979)
9. Bennett, Tony, et al. (eds), Culture, Ideology and Social Process (London: Batsford and Open University Press. 1983)
10. Bernstein, Basil, Class, Codes and Control, Vol III, 2nd edition (London: Routledge and Kegan Pual Ltd., 1975)
11. Bernstein, J.M., The Philosophy of the Novel (Minnesota: Minnesota University Press, 1984)
12. Bluhm, William Theodore, Ideologies and Attitudes (Englewood Cliffs: Prentice-Hall, 1974)
13. Bourdieu, R and Passeron, J.C., Reproduction in Education, Society and Culture, (London: Sage, 1977)
14. Bradbury, Malcolm. The Modern World: Ten Great Writers (London: Secker and Warburg, 1988)
15. Culler. Jonathan, Framing the Sign (Oxford: Basil Blackwell, 1988) Eagleton, Terry, The Ideology of the Aesthetic (Oxford: Basil Blackwell, 1990)

16. Literary Theory (Minneapolis: University of Minnesota Press, 1984)
17. Flint, Kate (ed), The Victorian Novelist: Social Problems and Social Change (London: Croom Helm, 1987)
18. Ford, Boris (ed), The new Pelican Guide to English Literature. Vol 6 (Reading: Cox and Wyman Ltd., 1983)
19. Giddens, Anthony, Central Problems in Social Theory (London: Macmillan Ltd., 1987) -Social Theory and Modern Sociology (London: Polity Press, 1987)
20. Goldman, Lucien, The Philosophy of the Enlightenment (London: Routledge and Kegan Paul Ltd., 1973) -The Hidden God (London: Routledge and Kegan Paul Ltd., 1964) transl. Philip Thody - Cultural Creation in Modern Society (Oxford: Basil Blackwell, 1977) transl. Bart Grahl.
21. Method and the Sociology of Literature (Oxford: Basil Blackwell, 1981) transl. William Boelhower.
22. Towards Sociology of the Novel (London: Tavistock Pub. Ltd., 1964)
23. Lukacs and Heidegger (Oxford: Basil Blackwell, 1977) transl. William Boelhower.
24. Harvey, David,-The Condition of Postmodernity (Oxford: Basil Blackwell Ltd., 1990)
25. Haug, Wolfgang, Commodity and Aesthetics, Ideology and Culture (New York: International General, 1987)
26. Hollingdale, R.J. transl. - A Nietzsche Reader (London: Penguin Books, 1977)
27. Inglis, Fred, Ideology and the Imagination (London: Cambridge University Press, 1975)
28. Kearney, Richard, Dialogues with Contemporary Continental Thinkers (Manchester: Manchester University Press, 1986)
29. Knight, David, The Age of Science (Oxford: Basil Blackwell, 1986)
30. Koelb, Clayton, (ed), Nietzsche as Postmodernist (New York: Suny Press, 1990)
31. Kuhn, Thomas, S., The Structure of Scientific Revolution (New York: New American Library, 1986) 2nd edition

32. Larrain, Jeorge, The Concept of Ideology (London: Hutchinson, 1979)
33. Lash, Scott and Urry, John, The End of Organised Capitalism (Oxford: Basil Blackwell Ltd., 1988)
34. Lavine, T.Z., From Socrates to Sartre: the Philosophic Quest (Toronto: Bantam Books, 1984)
35. Lechte, John, Julia Kristeva (London: Routledge, 1990)
36. Mannheim, Karl, Ideology, and Utopia: An introduction to the Sociology of Knowledge (London: Routledge and Kegan Paul, 1936) transl. Louis Wirth and Edward Shils.
37. Merleau-Ponty, Maurice, Adventures of the Dialectic (London: Heinemann Educ., 1974) transl. Joseph Bien.
38. Mishra, Ramesh, Society, and Social Policy (London: Macmillan Educ. Ltd, 1989) 2nd edition.
39. Nietzsche, Friedrich, On the Genealogy of Morals (Toronto: Vintage Books, 1969)
40. Human all too Human (London: Penguin Books, 1986) transl. R.J. Hollingdale
41. Beyond Good and Evil (London: George Allen and Unwin Ltd., 1967)
42. Norris, Christopher, The Deconstructive Turn: Essays in the Rhetoric of Philosophy (London: Routledge and Kegan Paul Ltd., 1989)
43. Nussbaum, Felicity A., The Autobiographical Subject (Baltimore: John Hopkins University Press, 1989)
44. Rabinow, Paul (ed), A Foucault Reader (New York: Penguin, 1984)
45. Ricoeur, Paul, The Conflict of Interpretations (Evanston: North-western University Press, 1974)
46. Rockwell, Joan Fact in Fiction (London: Routledge and Kegan Paul Ltd., 1974)
47. Rosaldo, Renato, Culture, and Truth: the remaking of Social Analysis (Boston, Beacon Press, 1989)
48. Routh, Jane and Wolff, J. (eds), The Sociology of Literature:
49. Theoretical Approaches (London: Wood-Mitchel & Co Ltd., 1977)

50. Saintsbury, George, A Short History of English Literature (London: Macmillan & co Ltd., 1913)
51. Samuel, Raphael, 'Workshop of the World' in History Workshop Journal (Issue 3, Spring 1917)
52. Smelser, Neil Je, The Sociology of Economic Life (Englewood Cliffs: Prentice-Hall, Inc., c. 1976) 2nd edition.
53. Thompson, J.B., Studies in the Theory of Ideology (London: Polity Press, 19984)
54. Thompson, Kenneth, Beliefs, and Ideology (Chichester: Ellis Horwood, 1986)
55. Ward, Benjamin, The Ideal Worlds of Economics (London: Macmillan, 1979)
56. Weber, Max, The Protestant Ethic and the Spirit of Capitalism (London: Unwin, 1930) transl. Talcott Parsons.
57. Whyte, Hayden V., The Content of Form (Baltimore: John Hopkins University Press, c 1987)
58. Williams, Raymond, Culture (Glasgow: Fontana, 1981)
59. Culture and Society (Hammondsworth: Penguin, 1977)
60. Wuthnow, Robert Meaning and Moral Order (Berkeley: Univ. of California Press, 1987)

9 789393 734549

Printed at Repro India Ltd.